THE
ART OF
EVERYTHING

connect your story
to History

/ hamilton
winters

THE ART OF EVERYTHING
connect your story to History
© 2022 by Hamilton Winters

Printed in the United States of America.
ISBN-13: 979-8-9854661-0-2
LCCN: 2021925276

Nebula Publishing
Atlanta, Georgia

NEBULA
publishing

table of contents

foreword

by Watts Dantzler

Like most of the stories in this book, the setting for my introduction to the author was slightly off. The best stories usually start on particularly odd foundations. A small voice told me, just play this situation out, take a chance, and see how it unfolds.

In February 2020, I walked through the doors of a Friday morning men's group for the first time. I arrived 15 minutes early and did not see the friend who invited me. By happenstance, I picked a random table on the outskirts of the room, and there sat Hamilton. He was already set up and ready to go, looking like a young college professor who had already downed two cups of coffee prepping for class to start.

I was in my second month of marathon training and walked in with my ego taking center stage. God had plenty of humbling moments planned for my life after this meeting. I did what most humans do when meeting someone. I judged the book by its cover. Hamilton was decked head to toe in black with plenty of matching tech-savvy accessories. He wore Lululemon joggers, and a Nike dri-fit shirt and hat. His coffee thermos and MacBook proudly displayed decals from Ole Miss, Louisiana, Monroe, and a distinct flight school logo.

While waiting for the rest of the group to arrive, we exchanged basic information with one another. I shared of my heavier days when I played offensive line for the University of Georgia. I asked about the flight school logo on his computer and his journey to Atlanta. I hate to say it, but my first instinct was that Hamilton was a spoiled, wannabe, know-it-all, trust-fund-baby Christian here to tell me how to live my life better.

When the friend who had invited me walked into the room, I told him I would give Hamilton's table a test run this week. I was curious how a 26-year-old had gained the knowledge, wisdom, and confidence to lead other men. Although Hamilton looked decent in the athletic jumpsuit, he certainly wouldn't have been the first person picked in a pickup basketball game. After watching Hamilton lead a one-hour-long discussion, I was hooked. He was the real deal.

Over the next seven months, I never missed a Friday morning. I saw why men twenty years older than

Hamilton were coming back each week to learn from him. He was incredibly gifted. Throughout that time, our group grew from 4 people to over 16, even during a global pandemic. Grown men were waking up at 6:30 every Friday morning to log onto a Zoom call just to join Hamilton's group. I quickly realized Hamilton was a strong spiritual pillar in every one of these guys' lives. I also began to believe the tracksuit I mocked him for wearing that first week might have been the only outfit he owned because he wore it every Friday as he poured life, love, and Jesus into every man God brought to our group. Hamilton became our spiritual Steve Jobs. He taught me that with less you can have so much more.

When I told Hamilton of my plans to run a 100-mile race that climbs over 13,000 ft of elevation, he said, "Watts, you're crazy. But we serve a God who is crazier and way more powerful than anything we can comprehend. I know you'll do it." Hamilton was one of the first people I texted after completing the Georgia Jewel 100 miler in 29 hours 45 minutes. Hamilton helped me grow more than any other influence I went to for advice as God transformed my life from who I was to whom He created me to be. Hamilton helped me share my story more effectively while pointing the glory to God for writing the script. It took a miracle for me to go from a 354 lb. obese alcoholic to a sober ultramarathon runner. Thankfully, we serve the God of miracles. It's my joy to help other people change their lives by passing on lessons I have learned from my failures. God wrote a storyline way more inspirational than anything I had planned for my life.

While reading this book, you will see how Hamilton's life journey is connected back to the story of Scripture. You will notice that God is still in the miracle business, and he uses them to teach us valuable lessons. When I think back to all the crazy connections that led me to the wrong small group table, that encounter is a testament to the type of author and creator God is. His work is brilliant and layered in a way we cannot understand. The twelve stories in this book will teach you how to appreciate your past while discovering new opportunities for God to use you in the future. It will encourage you to take chances and follow God when the path seems unclear.

A year into our friendship, Hamilton and I went with a men's group on a retreat in the mountains of North Carolina. Both of us recently became engaged to two of the loveliest ladies in the world and these life decisions set the stage for a deep discussion about our future and what else he and I wanted out of this life. Hamilton had just turned down a massive promotion at a marketing company he helped build. Any 26-year-old in the country would be crazy not to take the promotion and new job title. Hamilton made a seemingly foolish financial decision by choosing to go to seminary school instead of staying in the sales and marketing world. That day I realized Hamilton isn't concerned with making money. It's rare to meet someone who truly does not desire the treasures of this world. Instead, Hamilton is concerned with making an impact by furthering the Kingdom here on Earth. He knows that God will provide the rest.

Later that night, I asked Hamilton what his "Only God" dream was. An "Only God" dream is a vision that only God can accomplish in our lives. He paused for a second before responding.

"My only God dream is to be the most effective communicator of the Gospel in our generation." I chuckled and said, "Hamilton, you're crazy. But someone once told me we serve a God who is crazier and way more powerful than anything we can comprehend. I know you'll do it."

I could not have been more wrong about my first impression of Hamilton. He is one of the kindest, most intelligent, and most noble men I've ever had the privilege of meeting. He walks a path uncommon in our world. He loves as Jesus does. He meets people exactly where they are with open arms and listens to them. God continues to give Hamilton stages on which to shine for Jesus. Why? Because Hamilton has put in the hours required to be great and gives all of his talents and skills to the Lord. I look forward to running around the globe, following him to wherever he is speaking.

When you finish this book, you will see that Hamilton is well on his way to realizing his "only God" vision. God has him right where he needs to be. Hamilton once described the welcoming party he believes we get in Heaven. He painted a beautiful picture of entering through the pearly gates greeted by those we shared Jesus with during this life. I'm sure this book will add multitudes of people to Hamilton's party in Heaven. After you finish this book, please share it with someone you want to be a part of your Heavenly welcome party. People are all you can take to Heaven with you, and God's story is far too incredible to keep to yourself. Pass it on.

—Watts Byron Dantzler, Pass the Torch

preface

Hello, friend. Thank you for picking up this book today.

More than 140 million books exist in the world. Your choice to read this book today serves as one of the greatest compliments you could give me or anyone else, so thank you.

I have never professionally published my writings before. That said, I have no idea how this will turn out. My grandfather, the late Dr. Harry Winters, used to say, "Expectations are simply premeditated disappointments." So please know I hold no expectations beyond trusting that God will take this book as far as he sees fit.

This book comprises twelve personal and true stories which occurred throughout my time on this planet thus far. Each of my stories is paired with an ancient story from Scripture which bears a striking resemblance to mine. If the description of the book thus far doesn't interest you, that's okay. I'm with you. I read a lot, but not many books like this one. I hope you continue reading despite your skepticism. More often than not, I find myself pleasantly surprised on the other side of my hesitations if I see it through to the end.

Most folks wait for their lives to be nearly complete before they recount and share the events they've experienced and the lessons they've learned. I chose not to wait–not because I couldn't wait–but because none of us ever know when our lives are "complete."

I am 26 years old, so this book could be considered a quarter-life autobiography. But, just as easily, this book could be regarded as a full-life autobiography. I could die tomorrow, and had I not written these accounts, these stories would die with me. Would the world go on without them? Of course. But could lives be changed by telling them? Absolutely, and this is my hope.

There are a lot of questions in this world; however, one trumps them all. "What's the meaning of life?"

In other words, "Why are we here?"

This one, eternal question has plagued humanity since the very beginning. Even the most brilliant minds have had difficulty coming up with an answer to this question.

I'm not naive or arrogant enough to say I have the answer. I don't. But I think I have a clue.

None of us have the same story. But we all have a story. Like a heartbeat, you can't have life without a story.

The two are inseparable.

If life and stories are synonymous, is it foolish to think our stories might hold the key to answering the eternal question?

I don't believe in coincidences, so I don't find it difficult to believe God would use the one thing we all have in common—stories—to not only provide meaning for our lives, but that he would use a story of his own—Scripture—to bring us to himself.

If this is true, it's no wonder the enemy's #1 target is your story.

Jesus said, "The thief comes only to steal and kill and destroy. I came that they may have life and have it abundantly." John 10:10 NIV

The enemy wants to steal, kill, and destroy your story.

But he usually doesn't do it by causing horrible things to happen out of nowhere. Rather, he distracts you from being present and convinces you to settle for a mundane life while holding the idea of abundance out of your reach.

I cannot begin to tell you how many times the enemy has attempted to damper my story by telling me to keep quiet and be "normal." I can't tell you how many times he's whispered lies in my ear telling me I'm inadequate, I'm unremarkable, and my story doesn't matter. If you can relate to such noise, I wrote this book for you.

I'm a classically trained marketer. I always start a business relationship by attempting to understand the why behind what people do.

I intend to begin this relationship with you similarly. However, before you take this journey with me, you deserve complete transparency about the mission behind our travels.

This book exists to serve by entertaining you using unexplainable events that have happened in my life, educating you by giving an overview of a biblical account, and tying it in with my experience teaching you how to reflect and connect your story to God's story (History).

Do you know your purpose?

If you don't, that's okay. Unfortunately, some people spend their entire lives without genuinely discovering their reason for being.

In a world struggling with meaning, my obligation and duty as a Jesus follower is to share the purpose I have found in him. Christ is my reason. And Scripture is my story.

Throughout this book, you will read accounts both from my life and the lives of many Biblical characters. But although the experiences in this book might be my own, they aren't unique to me. You've had them too. I hope you will use the framework of this book to look back on your own experiences and begin connecting them to scriptural accounts as well. By doing so, you will start to notice that God is still writing his story through people just like you!

My goal with this book is to bridge the gap between two audiences:

Those who *know* the Bible but don't *live* it.

Those who *live* the Bible but don't *know* it.

Just because you might not know or notice the gospel in your life doesn't mean you haven't lived it. You have, and this book will show you how to connect the dots. Today, you become part of the bigger narrative. Today you become part of his story, or as it's commonly referred to, History.

Every story needs a starting point, and ours takes us back more than four thousand years. In the book of Genesis, God made an extraordinary promise to a man named Abraham to bless him and make his descendants as numerous as the stars in the sky and the sand on the seashore (Genesis 22:16-18). Not only was Abraham in his nineties at the time, but his wife, Sarah, had been barren all her life.

This promise is the backdrop of every story within this book, so keep it in mind as we trace through time and space together. Spoiler alert: God—just as he always does—has made and is still making good on his promise to Abraham. How he does it, we are about to find out.

Your story + my story = History

"...the powerful play goes on, and you may contribute a verse."

"O Me! O Life!" By Walt Whitman

acknowledgments

I t is said a certain level of craziness is required to write a book. If this is true, said person requires a tribe of people around them who are willing to walk alongside them both in the best and in the worst days of this process. Thankfully, God has blessed me with such a tribe.

None of the accounts contained within, or the book itself would have been possible without the support and encouragement of the following people:

Mom and Dad, thank you for the two greatest gifts you have ever given me: my life and my faith. Also, thank you for trusting me in situations other parents would have questioned. Had you not, most of these stories would not exist and I would not be the person I am today. I love you.

To the love of my life, Alix, thank you for your constant encouragement, reassurance, and unconditional love. You embody Jesus more than anyone I know, and I can't wait for the journey that lies ahead of us in marriage. I hope our kids are just like you.

Hollin and Hallie, thank you for being the greatest cheerleaders and sisters I could have ever asked for, and for listening to and accepting my advice even if you don't take it.

To my grandmother, Joyce Barnes, thank you for investing your love and your time in me. You will never know how much hearing your voice on the other end of a phone call means to me.

Trevor and Kathryn Smith, thank you for bringing me to Atlanta and opening your hearts and lives to me. Thank you also for giving me one of the greatest joys of my life thus far, your son Ryder. I can't wait to see how God uses all three of you in the future. Alix and I are forever grateful for your friendship and love.

Russell Pizzuto, thank you for giving me the opportunity of a lifetime. I will always cherish the days we spent together building NSPIRE Aviation. I couldn't have asked for a better friend or business partner.

Tucker Yates, thank you for being uncommon and making a place for men in Atlanta, like me, to not only grow in our faith but to share with and lead other men to know and make Jesus known. God has certainly placed you in your royal position for such a time as this.

Gus Bueno, thank you for every early morning coffee meeting over the past few years, and for continuing to ask me about the progress of my book even when I was ashamed to answer. Had it not been for your prompting and prodding, this book would not have come to fruition as it did. I am forever grateful.

Watts Dantzler, thank you for writing the foreword in this book and inspiring me and spurring me on toward greatness in Christ. It is one thing to inspire. It is another thing to be equally inspired by someone you inspire. You are a hero of mine, and although God has used you in mighty ways thus far, I cannot wait to see how he uses you to change the world in the future. I hope to be by your side for it all. You are the ticket.

Whitney Barnes Baker, thank you for your help on the book cover. Your eye for design and gift for artistic creativity amazes me. I'm thankful to be your cousin, but more so your friend.

Nancy Counts, Kathy Hart, Mary Bernard, Heather Gulde, and Dr. Glenn Kreider, thank you for taking the time and putting in the effort to proofread and provide feedback on this book before its publication. Your edits and insight are invaluable to me, and I am honored to be a student of yours.

To all the people named within the chapters of this book, thank you for playing an integral role in my life. You each hold a very special place in my heart, and I cherish the memories we've made together.

Finally, thank *you* for reading this book. Every author wonders who, if anyone, will read their book, and if what they have to say will have an impact on the reader's life. Whether I know you personally or not, I have prayed continuously for you since the inception of this book. You are a blessing to me, and I pray this book blesses you in return.

how to read this book

At a friend's advice, I decided to add this short section called "How to Read This Book." I am fully confident in your ability to read a book—this book in particular— however, I wrote this book a bit differently than other books you might have read.

As you read, you'll notice each chapter title following the same format. All twelve chapter titles start with "The Art of" and end with a mundane action. Each represents an experience you might live or behaviors you might perform on a semi-regular basis. The first half of each chapter begins with an account from my own life where something extraordinary happens in otherwise ordinary circumstances related to the title. The second half contains an overview of a Bible story that parallels my own. Five discussion questions follow each chapter under the acronym "F.A.V.O.R" to continue the conversation.

"F" – Foundation – the foundational Bible verse for the chapter.

"A" – Application – how you apply the story to your life.

"V" – Vision – be intentional in using what you learn from the chapter in future opportunities or circumstances.

"O" – Orientation – Fill in the blank. I can share this story with _____ today.

"R" – Reflection – Look back on your life for experiences that parallel the biblical account referenced in the chapter.

While I aim to show you a new way to approach both today and tomorrow, I also intend to provide an alternative perspective to the events and experiences of yesterday. Every single event and occasion you've ever lived contributed to you becoming who you are.

Based on the fact that you're alive and reading this book right now, God still has plans to use you. Reflecting on how God has shaped you in the past allows you to glimpse how God intends to use you in the present and future.

History is your story too. I hope the following twelve chapters prove that to you.

1
the art of sleeping late

In January 2009, a middle-school leadership conference sent me an invitation to attend the presidential inauguration of Barack Obama. Honored, I accepted the invitation. Millions of people descended on the Capitol for this historic event. As a thirteen-year-old, I relished the opportunity to witness history unfold before my eyes.

I grew up around politics. My father, Stephens Winters, works as a state district court judge in Louisiana. My grandmother, Mary Lou Winters, served as former chairwoman of the Democratic Party of Louisiana and DNC superdelegate. I was too young to vote at the time; however, I understood the significance of the first African American president of the United States.

The inauguration did not disappoint. Throughout the week, world leaders such as former Vice President Al

Gore, General Colin Powell, reporter Lisa Ling, and Reverend Desmond Tutu addressed our teenage congregation. On inauguration day, a security guard mistakenly admitted one of my peers and me into the "gold" section of the National Mall. The rest of our group stood more than a mile away, viewing the event on a Jumbotron while my friend and I stood less than a hundred yards from the steps of the Capitol.

To cap off the end of a fantastic week, our conference hosted a black-tie gala at the Smithsonian Museum of Air and Space. The gala lasted until 4:00 AM. My flight out the following day departed at 10:30 AM from Dulles International Airport. So, I needed to leave the hotel by 7:30 AM at the latest.

The following day, I woke up to a strange sensation, which I can only describe as a kind of 'tap' on my shoulder. I looked to see who woke me, but I found myself alone. Oddly, I felt well-rested even though I slept so little the night before.

I glanced at the alarm clock. Horrified, the truth of the matter hit me. It was 11:30 AM. I had missed my flight by more than an hour. I frantically called my mom to break the bad news. Her calm reaction on the other end of the line still serves as an example of how to handle a crisis.

"Don't worry, "she said, "We'll make plans for you to get home, but don't waste your day. See this as a blessing. Make the most of it."

"What is my first move?" I asked myself silently. Think Hamilton, think. Throughout the past week, the editor of our local newspaper, Greg, called daily to document my experience at the inauguration. I thought to myself, "Greg is going to love this." I remembered talking to him earlier in the week, and he passed the phone to our family friend, Congressman Rodney Alexander.

"I hope you're enjoying Washington," the congressman said. "If you need anything, don't hesitate to call me." Bingo.

I immediately made two phone calls. First, I called Greg to fill him in on the plotline's breaking details and ask for Congressman Alexander's contact information. Then, I called Congressman Alexander to ask his advice as to my next move.

"Get a cab, come toward the Capitol, and I'll meet you at the Cannon House Office Building. I'll have my chief of staff meet you downstairs," said Congressman Alexander.

I briskly packed my things and headed downstairs to the lobby of our hotel. Not knowing where I would stay that night, the hotel concierge allowed me to store my luggage for the time being. I hailed a cab and headed to the Capitol.

I love talking to cab drivers. During the thirty-minute drive to the Capitol, I discovered my driver was from Uganda. We held a great conversation about family, faith, and his journey to the United States. Arriving at my destination, I asked for my fare. "Fifteen dollars and eighty-five cents, please." Reaching into my back pocket, I found no wallet.

Sheer terror. Could this day get any worse?

Not only did I find myself a 13-year-old stranded in Washington, D.C. alone, but now I have no money and no ID card to return home. My whole life felt as if it were coming to a screeching halt.

"Sir, I don't know how to tell you this, but I don't have my wallet on me. I must have left it at the hotel," I said.

The cab driver responded, "You're kidding, right?"

I wish. I pleaded with the cab driver to take me back to the hotel in hopes that my wallet would be there. If it wasn't, I had no other form of payment.

After some consideration, the reluctant cab driver graciously agreed to drive me back to the hotel. From the back of his Lincoln Town car, I called the hotel and frantically prayed, "Please pick up. Please pick up." Finally, the receptionist transferred me to the same concierge who helped me store my luggage.

"Let me check our lost and found, Mr. Winters," she said, putting me on hold for a few agonizing minutes.

"Mr. Winters, good news. The bellhop found your wallet on a chair. We have it for you here at the front desk."

I let out a massive sigh of relief. Hope in the middle of hopelessness. At least one thing turned out alright so far today. I wasn't back to par yet, but I was well on my way.

Maybe the wallet started a new trend for the day.

Exiting the cab at the office building, I generously tipped my new friend and thanked him for his patience. Just as expected, Congressman Alexander's chief of staff waited outside for my arrival. Without explanation or excuse, I apologized for being a bit tardy.

After going through security, the chief of staff instructed me to wait for the congressman in his office. "We've all been following your trip in the paper this week. It looks like you've had a lot of fun," he said to me. "Sounds like today has been pretty wild, though." He reached in his back pocket and handed me a folded sheet of copy paper.

Opening it, I recognized the front page of my hometown newspaper. "Winters Stranded in Washington" was the headline. Wow. It's like the newspaper knew before I did. I wish they would have clued me in, I thought to myself.

A few minutes later, Congressman Alexander greeted me with a warm handshake. "We're going to have a great day together, you and me," he said. "Have you ever toured the Capitol?"

"Never," I said. But this was a white lie.

I toured the Capitol a couple of years before on a school trip. I rarely lied, but I didn't want the congressman to skip over parts that I had already seen, so I acted as if it was my first time.

We walked from place to place, admiring the art and architecture of the building.

"I'm about to have to duck back into the session. I have a vote coming up on the floor soon. How would you like to cast it for me?" asked the congressman.

"It would be an honor, sir."

Still unsure as to my plans for the evening, I got a phone call from my mom.

"I hope you've had a great day! Do you happen to remember a lady named Barbara whose daughter you used to go to school with?"

I remembered her well.

"I just got a phone call from her. She works with Greg as chief editor of the newspaper. Did you know your grandfather was the doctor who delivered her when she was born?"

I had no idea.

"She said her parents know Paw Paw very well. They live in Arlington, Virginia, and have been following your trip this week. They would like to take you out to dinner tonight and have offered for you to stay at their home tonight. They're on their way to pick you up now."

That evening, Mr. and Mrs. Griggs, Barbara's parents, picked me up and took me to an incredible seafood restaurant. They treated me like a prince. The Griggs and I had so much fun together that evening.

What a day.

The following morning, I found myself on a flight home from my wild journey to Washington. What an adventure! A nightmare of a day paved the way for dreams to come true.

In the book of Genesis, we meet a character named Joseph. Joseph was the eleventh of twelve sons of Jacob, grandsons of Isaac, and great-grandsons of Abraham. Joseph found himself the most favored of all of his father's sons. As a token of his affection, Jacob fashioned a coat of many colors for Joseph. The brothers seethed in anger.

Joseph saw visions in dreams that his family would one day bow to him. When he revealed the revelations to his family, his brothers plotted to kill him. Reuben, the eldest of the brothers, suggested that rather than kill Joseph, they should instead sell him as a slave to the Egyptian merchants passing by. Smearing goat blood on Joseph's coat, the brothers returned home to their father, convincing him that Joseph was dead.

Upon arrival in Egypt, Joseph was re-sold to the captain of Pharaoh's guard, Potiphar. Not long after, Potiphar's wife tried to seduce Joseph into sleeping with her. When Joseph refused her repeated advances, she falsely accused Joseph of raping her, landing Joseph in prison.

Pharaoh's cupbearer and baker were also in prison at the time. Both men experienced dreams and asked Joseph to interpret them. In exchange for remembering him in his time of need, Joseph interpreted both dreams to mean Pharaoh would restore the cupbearer to his position and remove the baker's head. When Joseph's predictions came true, the cupbearer forgot about Joseph.

Two years later, Pharaoh had a dream no one in Egypt was able to interpret. The cupbearer remembered and recommended Joseph. Pharaoh immediately summoned Joseph to interpret his dream.

Joseph correctly interpreted Pharaoh's dream to mean that Egypt would soon experience seven years of excess followed by seven years of famine. Pharaoh needed to appoint a responsible man to facilitate the storage and management of surplus grain. Impressed by Joseph's ability to interpret visions, Pharaoh appointed Joseph to this position, making Joseph, a Hebrew, his prime minister, the second most powerful man in Egypt.

During the seven years of famine, Egypt became the only nation in the region with grain to eat. With his people starving in Canaan, Jacob sent his sons to Egypt to purchase food. The brothers arrived in Egypt and stood before Joseph. The brothers did not recognize him, but Joseph recognized his brothers barely refraining from weeping. Joseph used an interpreter to prevent revealing his identity.

Joseph noticed his younger brother, Benjamin, was not with the group. Rather than sell them grain, Joseph accused his brothers of being spies and placed them in prison. The brothers pleaded with Joseph and admitted their youngest brother, Benjamin, was still at home. Joseph demanded that the brothers bring Benjamin to Egypt, and placed Simeon in his custody until the brothers returned with Benjamin.

Devising a clever plan, Joseph secretly sneaks a silver cup into Benjamin's grain sack. Shortly after leaving Egypt, Joseph sends stewards out to investigate. They find the silver cup in Benjamin's bag, forcing the brothers to return to Egypt in shame. Judah explained the situation honestly and pleaded with Joseph to punish him instead of Benjamin for the crime. Seeing the brothers' devotion toward Benjamin and the remorse over their actions, Joseph finally revealed his identity to his astonished siblings.

Following this heartfelt reunion, Pharaoh invited Jacob and his entire family to settle in Egypt. This series of events sets the stage for the Hebrews' ultimate enslavement in Egypt and their subsequent exodus after the plagues.

Joseph recounted his trials with his brother by saying, "You intended to harm me, but God intended it for good to accomplish what is now being done, the saving of many lives." Genesis 50:20 NIV

While nowhere close in scope or scale to the misfortunes of Joseph, my Washington experience allowed me to understand Joseph better. At one point in Joseph's life, it seemed as if nothing was going right.

Despised by his brothers, sold into slavery, accused of rape, thrown in prison, and forgotten by those he helped to free, it was difficult for Joseph to see God using his circumstances for good.

On that fateful January morning, I had no way to get home, no plan of action, no wallet, and nowhere to lay my head. I found it difficult to see God using my circumstances for good, too. But, by the end of the day, I had toured the US Capitol, cast a vote on the congressional floor, feasted on a seafood spread, and spent the night in a turned-down bed in a cozy Arlington, Virginia home.

The events which seemed to harm me God used to pave the way for one of the most fortunate days I can remember. Only God could use nightmares to make dreams come true.

F.A.V.O.R. DISCUSSION QUESTIONS
CHAPTER 1

Foundation: Genesis 50:19-20 NIV "But Joseph said to them, "Don't be afraid. Am I in the place of God? You intended to harm me, but God intended it for good to accomplish what is now being done, the saving of many lives.""

Application: How are you overcoming adversity like Joseph?

Vision: When facing adversity in the future, how will you use it to make an impact or even save lives?

Orientation: To whom in your life is this story relevant? Write their name down and share it with them.

Name: _____

Reflection: Think back on your life. How does one of your life experiences connect with Joseph?

2
the art of watching a parade

Each year, my family visits New Orleans, Louisiana for Mardi Gras as part of a tradition dating back for many years. Festivities begin as early as three weeks before actual "Fat Tuesday." We typically spend the weekend leading up to Mardi Gras celebrating with my father's extended family living in the New Orleans area.

Regular Mardi Gras attendees know traditions do not change much from year to year. You typically go to the same parades at the same times on the same days and stand in the same spot on the same street with the same people year after year. The corner of St. Charles and Conery in Uptown is our spot.

For those who have never experienced Mardi Gras in Uptown New Orleans before, here's a brief explanation of how it works:

St. Charles Avenue stretches for seven miles from the bank of the Mississippi River to the French Quarter in downtown. One of America's most beautiful streets, stately southern mansions line each side with the two-railed famous New Orleans streetcars between. During Mardi Gras, the south lane of St. Charles remains open to pedestrians and limited auto traffic. The north lane of St. Charles represents the designated parade route. Everyone sets up for the parade in what's referred to as the "neutral zone," where streetcars typically run. Tens of thousands of people line both sides of the avenue for the parades each year, yelling, "Throw me something, mister!" to the folks riding the floats. These riders belong to a "krewe" or the social group responsible for their respective parade.

My late grandmother, Mary Lou Winters, was a veteran member of the "Krewe of Iris." We chose the corner of St. Charles and Conery because it sits near the end of Iris's route, and my grandmother would toss all of the grandchildren a boatload of beads she had saved for us.

During Mardi Gras, the crowd is entirely random. This randomness lowers your perception to notice novelty, but it also heightens your perception of consistency. Each year there was one notable consistency. His name is Bowdre.

Mardi Gras 2015 found me as a sophomore at the University of Louisiana at Monroe. As always, my family and friends accompanied me to the parades that year. My now late grandfather and some distant cousins of ours also attended. We popped the tailgate tent, opened the lawn chairs, and set up our ladders for the parade.

More explanation here. When you go to Mardi Gras, expect to see thousands of ladders lining the streets up against the parade route. The Mardi Gras ladder is an ingenious invention by the people of Louisiana. Parade-goers convert typical six-foot ladders into a multi-use tool for catching beads. Drilling a wooden toolbox to the top of the ladder makes for a seat with a handrail for a child. The parent stands on the ladder steps behind their child to protect the child when catching beads. The paint bucket holder underneath serves as a hanger for bead bags where catches are stored. Wheels are installed on each side of the toolbox, and collapsing it makes for an easy roll to and from the car. Ladders bear the traditional colors of Mardi Gras: purple, green, and gold, or a combination of the three.

As we completed our setup, my father and I noticed an older man sitting at the base of a giant live oak tree on the corner of St. Charles and Conery Streets. He wore a red zippered jacket over a green apron covering a faded blue jumpsuit, white tube socks, and khaki-colored sneakers. A veteran's hat on his head, a pair of glasses on his face, and one strand of beads featuring the flag of each respective military branch hung around his neck. He sat on a stack of newspapers instead of a chair. Obviously, he was not attending to catch beads. He showed up to observe the festivities and celebrate the life around him.

Dad and I had seen him before, but we had never introduced ourselves. Approaching the man, we asked him his name. "My name is Bowdre." We inquired as to his age and background. Bowdre told us he was a 91-year-old World War II veteran.

Upholding his vow of secrecy from more than seven decades ago, he wouldn't tell us much about his role in the war; however, he did refer us to a YouTube video made about his unit. We discovered Bowdre served as an elite Japanese code breaker in the Pacific Theater. His team was responsible for breaking the enigma of enemy communications to foil plots, inform allies, and ultimately win the war against the Japanese Empire.

We were amazed. Bowdre's humility, loyalty, and heroism were apparent as much today as ever. He volunteers as a tour guide at the United States World War II Museum in New Orleans, where students and tourists learn about the horrors and heroes of the great war from a participant and legend of freedom.

Our conversation with Bowdre drew the attention of others in the vicinity. One after another, onlookers joined in our discussion as we explained that we were in the presence of a hero. Bowdre spent the day being celebrated by a crowd of folks who at one time passed him by without notice.

Nearly everyone in attendance of a Mardi Gras parade stands as close to the street edge as possible to catch a glimpse of the floats passing by. Maybe, if they're lucky, they'll catch a few throws too. Bowdre discovered his spot away from the crowd offered a much more valuable perspective. Bowdre's decision to do what no one else was doing brought him to our attention and made Bowdre our friend.

In the Gospel of Luke, we meet the wealthy chief tax collector of the town of Jericho. His name was Zacchaeus. As Jesus entered Jericho, crowds swarmed to see him. Many people laid eyes on Jesus that day, but many more did not because of the large crowd. Zacchaeus was short, so he had difficulty seeing Jesus.

Instead of fighting his way through the crowd, Zacchaeus decided to find another spot for viewing. Zacchaeus famously climbed a sycamore-fig tree for a different perspective. Seeing the man in the tree, Jesus calls Zacchaeus by name and asks him to stay at his house for the day. Zacchaeus humbly obliges.

Zacchaeus made it into the Bible, not because of the quality of his character, but because of the effort, he made to see Jesus from a different perspective.

Had Bowdre viewed the parade from the same spot as everyone else, we would have never noticed him. Bowdre made watching the parades an art form by sitting where no one else was seated. That decision rewarded him with a perspective that no one else received and caused our paths to cross.

Since that day, my family has remained in close contact with Bowdre. At the time of writing, Bowdre is alive and well in an assisted living home in McComb, MS. He is as mentally sharp and witty today as he has ever been.

The strand of beads he was wearing that day in 2015 hangs on my childhood bedroom door. It is one of my most prized possessions—a token of love and appreciation from my friend Bowdre.

More on this story to come at the conclusion of this book. Stay tuned.

F.A.V.O.R. DISCUSSION QUESTIONS
CHAPTER 2

Foundation: Luke 19:3-6 NIV "He wanted to see who Jesus was, but because he was short he could not see over the crowd. So he ran ahead and climbed a sycamore-fig tree to see him, since Jesus was coming that way. When Jesus reached the spot, he looked up and said to him, "Zacchaeus, come down immediately. I must stay at your house today." So he came down at once and welcomed him gladly."

Application: How are you changing your perspective like Zacchaeus?

Vision: What are your weaknesses? How will you overcome them in the future when the world is standing in your way?

Orientation: To whom in your life is this story relevant? Write their name down and share it with them.

Name: _____

Reflection: Think back on your life. How does one of your experiences connect with Zacchaeus?

3

the art of going through airport security

On August 6, 2017, I embarked upon my first journey to the Far East. I planned the entire trip myself with destinations including Beijing, Shanghai, Hong Kong, Tokyo, Bangkok, Bali, Sydney, and New Zealand. I had already booked and paid for flights and hotel rooms, but I had no daily plans in any of the locations.

Early on a Sunday morning, I found myself the only passenger inside the International Concourse of Atlanta's Hartsfield-Jackson International Airport. After checking in, I walked to the security gate, where a TSA agent greeted me with a surprisingly big smile and bubbly attitude. "Where are you headed, sweetie?" she said in a flirtatious tone.

"I'm going to China today," I replied, playing along with her.

"Is that right?" the woman said with an inflection in her tone, "Well, you best come back and tell me how it was over there!"

I agreed, gave her a warm hug, and went on my way toward the x-ray machines.

A layover in Toronto, Canada, was all that stood between Beijing and me. The weather forecast was clear, so there shouldn't be any unexpected hiccups. I arrived at Toronto Pearson International Airport on time for my next flight. I was supposed to have a two-hour layover; however, the departure board in the concourse read, "BEIJING - DELAYED 6:55 PM." It was currently 1:30 PM, so I'd need to get comfortable for a while.

Time passed slowly. About an hour before the flight's departure, the line began to form. Once the line started moving, I decided to call my mom one final time before takeoff. As I was talking to my mother, I heard a message come over the intercom. Thankfully I was wearing only one of my earbuds to listen to the announcement coming over the intercom.

As soon as the voice began to speak, I felt the same strange kind of 'tap' on my shoulder as I did that morning when I found myself stranded in Washington,

D.C. many years earlier. It's not a physical tap, but it is very recognizable. Each time I feel it, something life-changing is about to occur.

The announcement said, "Attention Air Canada passengers for flight 31 service to Beijing. Please have your identification cards and visa certificates visible at the gate to speed up the boarding process. Thank you."

Although I didn't know why, I felt I needed to inquire about this announcement based on the 'tap.' I told my mom I'd call her back, and I walked toward the gate desk.

Five Air Canada staff members greeted me as I walked up to the counter. The manager of the group said, "Hello, sir. How can we help you today?"

"You announced something about identification cards and visa certificates just now. I wanted to make sure I have everything squared away," I responded.

"Of course, sir. May I please see your passport?"

He flipped through the book once, then twice, and finally a third time. His casual scrolling turned to frantic searching for a page with my Chinese visa attached to it.

"Sir, you don't have a visa to get into China," he said, "where are you coming from?"

Before I could answer, one of his co-workers answered for me in shock. "He came from Atlanta."

He looked me dead in the eyes and said, "Security should have caught this mistake in Atlanta and never let you board your flight to Toronto. Sir, you've just entered Canada illegally."

Immediately my mind shifted to the flirtatious TSA Agent at the security checkpoint in Atlanta. Now that I recall, she was much more interested in me and my trip than my documentation. I'm not sure she ever even looked at my passport.

"Well, if I need a visa to get to China, can I get one here?"

Laughing, he replied, "Yes, but it will be complicated. You will need to visit the Chinese Consulate downtown tomorrow and apply for an expedited visa. This process takes a minimum of two weeks."

I had only planned to be in mainland China for six days. My trip seemed ruined.

Side note: I had done a fair deal of international traveling to this point (10 countries), and not a single country I had visited to this point required a visa for entry. I always received my visa at the gate upon entry. I had also spent countless hours researching my trip, memorizing protocols, learning local etiquette, and picking up travel tricks. I must have missed the part where they said I needed a visa to visit China.

"What are my options?" I asked.

He replied, "Well, how long is your trip?" "36 days," I answered.

Nervous, he responded, "I'd say your best option is to enjoy Toronto for a few days before booking your flight home. Or you could talk to the concierge across the hallway to see if they can help you in any way. Either way, I am sorry for this inconvenience, sir. None of us has ever seen anything like this."

I thanked them all before I walked away. I made it no farther than 15 feet from their desk before turning around for one final question.

"So, humor me here," I said. "I caught myself making this mistake. You guys were going to let me on that plane if I hadn't. What would have happened if I had boarded that plane and arrived in China without a visa?" "Do you want to know?" he asked.

"You would have spent the next 13 hours and 20 minutes on an airplane as excited and happy as could be. You would have landed in Beijing ready to explore but would have to go through customs first." He paused before continuing.

"Sir, based on what we know about Chinese immigration policy, the customs agent would have looked through your documents as I just did. Unable to find a visa, they would have called for backup. You would have noticed other officers coming toward your customs portal to discuss your documents. They would have likely handcuffed you in front of the crowd and taken you into a holding room for hours of questioning. Thinking you are a spy; they would then interrogate you about your motives for coming to China without permission and carrying only a backpack. When and if they concluded that you are a tourist, not a spy, you would be forced to pay your fare back to the US. As a penalty, customs would likely ban your entry into China for a minimum of 10 years."

Stunned, I realized this could have been my reality. Instead, here I sat, safe in Toronto, upset about my upended travel plans. Little did I know, God had just delivered me from this fate, yet I was acting like a brat about it. Talk about being humbled.

On my way to the concierge desk, I called my mom back to give her an update.

"Well, mom, it looks like my trip might not be happening, but boy, do I have a story for you."

I explained the situation briefly before ending the call to speak with an Air Canada representative. Before voicing my request, I prayed, "Lord, I don't know what is going to happen, but I trust in your will. Send me where You want me to go."

"Hello, sir. How are you today?" the Air Canada representative asked.

"Well, I'm kind of in a pickle. You see, I have a ticket on the flight to Beijing taking off right now, but I was unaware I needed a visa to enter China. Your co-workers at the gate told me I entered Canada illegally, and now I don't know what to do."

Trying to hold back her laugh, she said, "That is a new one. I'm sorry to hear about your misfortune, sir. I don't know what, if anything, I can do, but I am happy to help you find a solution, if possible."

The concierge asked for my passport and inquired about my travel plans.

"Sir, how long was your trip supposed to be? I see here that you have a one-way ticket to Beijing with no returning flight."

"It was going to be 36-days," I answered.

"I see. And what other destinations would you be visiting?" the concierge asked.

"After Beijing was Shanghai, then Hong Kong, Tokyo,Bangkok, Ba—..."

Cutting me off, she asked, "Did you say Hong Kong?"

Confused, I responded, "Yes, ma'am."

"Just a moment," she said as she picked up the phone to make a call.

Nearly ten minutes later, she returned.

"Sir, Hong Kong does not require a visa since it is an exclusionary zone of China. There is a chance we could get you to Hong Kong later in the week. Possibly Thursday or Friday. Would that be okay?" she asked.

It was Sunday. Thursday or Friday seemed like a long way away, but it could potentially salvage the majority of my trip.

"That would be wonderful," I answered.

"I must warn you; it will likely be costly to change your flight since it would be a completely new ticket issued close to the date of departure."

"I understand," I said. "Thank you."

"Of course. One moment," she said, picking up the phone to make another call.

The second call seemed to take an eternity but was likely only a bit longer than the first. Waiting in agony, I reminded myself that I was in no hurry. I didn't have a plan anymore. I was on God's time now.

I will never forget the facial expression the Air Canada representative wore as she walked back toward me. I couldn't read it for sure, but I assumed that it was not good news.

"Sir, I don't know how to say this, but you must be the luckiest person in the world."

"Hold on a minute. The luckiest person in the world?

Who is your source?!" I thought to myself.

I felt the exact opposite of lucky. Today seemed to be one of the unluckiest days in recent memory, but now the Air Canada concierge is telling me I'm the luckiest person in the world. How could that be?

"Well, sir. I just spoke with my manager. He said it is our fault for letting you into Canada in the first place. We should have caught the mistake in Atlanta. That said, we just reserved the last open seat on tomorrow morning's flight to Hong Kong for you. We are also providing you with a hotel room and meal vouchers for dinner tonight and breakfast tomorrow morning."

Handing me a small envelope, she said, "Inside is your boarding pass and hotel room key. Your flight leaves at 10:30 AM tomorrow. Please arrive at least two hours before departure time."

She then motioned toward a man standing in the hallway, saying, "My colleague here will escort you through the freight elevator to the hotel shuttle. Again, I am so sorry for the inconvenience caused to you today. I hope you understand and accept our apology."

Completely overwhelmed, I walked on the other side of the desk and gave her one of the biggest hugs I had ever given anyone in my life.

"Thank you," I said. "You have no idea what you've just done for me. God bless you."

I picked up my bags from baggage claim before heading to the hotel. Weeks before my departure, I planned to document my trip via Facebook Live videos. I had not filmed one to date, but I knew Facebook sent out notifications when people recorded their first.

My original plan was to film my first video from Beijing's Tiananmen Square; however, that was my plan. God planned to have me film my first video in hotel room 304 at the Crowne Plaza Toronto Airport Hotel.

I titled it, "You won't believe this."

Who knows how many people would have seen the video in Beijing? We will never know. My best estimate would probably be around a thousand. Instead, I filmed my first Facebook Live video in a Toronto hotel room as I recounted my crazy day and the beauty of God's divine protection. The video received just shy of ten thousand views within 24 hours. It also made the rest of the trip wildly popular on Facebook, drawing more than a thousand views to every video I recorded from that point forward.

Who would have heard the goodness of God that night had I landed safely in Beijing? I guess that Beijing, China, would have been the center of the storyline rather than God.

We will never know how many people would have watched the rest of my videos had the first one gone as planned. What we do know is that God had a much bigger story to tell than "Tiananmen Square is beautiful," "I made it to China," or "First stop: Beijing!" God's storyline was "My will trumps yours," "A little faith goes a long way," or most appropriate, "I will never leave you, nor forsake you."

The following day, I boarded my flight and departed for Hong Kong. The trip from that point forward was magnificent.

Providence kept me from visiting a place I longed to go, but only because God knew his story would travel further if I could not reach it.

One of the most famous books in the Bible is Paul's letter to the Romans. An apostle named Paul wrote this letter and the majority of the New Testament books. Paul longed to visit Rome, yet he found himself unable to reach the great city for various reasons.

Paul never asks God to open up the way for him to visit Rome. Instead, Paul provides a beautiful example of Godly prayer by asking, seeking, and knocking when one does not know God's specific will.

"...not my will, but yours be done." Luke 22:42 NIV

Years later, Paul did eventually reach Rome. Unfortunately, in Rome, Paul was beheaded for his faith in Christ. Paul's martyrdom for the cause of Christ made his story even more credible and encouraging to the people of Rome and beyond.

The same God who hindered Paul's journey could have easily allowed him to visit Rome on his first attempt. Instead, God blocked Paul's path to Rome, paving the way for billions of people throughout the world to read the letter Paul wrote to the Romans because he was unable to visit them in person.

Paul serves as a beautiful example that God's will is ultimate and that God's plans are much greater than yours. What seems to be God's hand against you could be what saves you and paves the way to tell his story in a much more impactful way than you ever thought possible.

F.A.V.O.R. DISCUSSION QUESTIONS
CHAPTER 3

Foundation: Romans 1:11-13 NIV "I long to see you so that I may impart to you some spiritual gift to make you strong— that is, that you and I may be mutually encouraged by each other's faith. I do not want you to be unaware, brothers and sisters, that I planned many times to come to you (but have been prevented from doing so until now) in order that I might have a harvest among you, just as I have had among the other Gentiles."

Application: How do you envision your plans changing today?

Vision: When plans go awry in the future, how will you respond?

Orientation: To whom in your life is this story relevant? Write their name down and share it with them.

Name: _____

Reflection: Think back on your life. How does one of your experiences connect with Paul's journey to Rome?

4
the art of climbing stairs

I originally planned to spend only three days in Hong Kong, but thanks to my updated travel arrangements, I ended up spending more than a week there. I affectionately referred to my extra time in Hong Kong as "icing days," as in the icing on the cake.

I never doubted that God sent me to Hong Kong for a reason; I just didn't know what that reason was yet. I would soon learn.

Each day, I met strangers who felt like long-time friends in what seemed like random occurrences during my walkabouts. These interactions opened the door for me to share my life and faith with them. God reminded me that, had my plans been honored, I never would have crossed their paths.

I find that I meet far more friends when I travel alone because it forces me to look for others with whom to engage. When I travel with friends or family, I interact with the group I brought with me rather than the multitude of possible connections all around me. Hong Kong, of all places, is a fantastic setting for meeting new people since they do not eat alone.

If you've visited Hong Kong before, you'll know there are escalators everywhere. The most famous set of escalators is known as the Central-Mid-Levels escalators. This escalator system stretches more than 800 meters (2,624 feet) in length and ascends an elevation of over 135 meters (443 feet) from bottom to top, making it the lengthiest covered escalator system in the world. Riders enter and exit the escalators at various points using stair ramps on each side street. These side streets contain a variety of local shops, restaurants, bars, etc.

Hong Kong is known for its "dim sum," small plates of dumplings and other traditional Cantonese snacks. On my way up the escalators, I spotted a particular dim sum restaurant with a line out the door. So, I exited the escalators and took my spot in line.

As I said earlier, in Hong Kong, no one eats alone. Real estate is exceptionally tight in Hong Kong. Restaurants must be tiny and compact to afford to operate. An individual patron would take up too much valuable real estate if he sat at a table alone, so the host seats him at any empty chair he can find. Either way, I am a solo traveler, and this fact made mealtimes prime for introductions.

Many people in Hong Kong speak English. Many more do not. Each interaction becomes a crapshoot of whether I can communicate or not. Fortunately, everyone with whom I came into contact over my first few days could speak at least conversational English. At this restaurant, the hostess placed me with two women of Asian descent, one middle-aged and the other noticeably younger. They both spoke fluent English, and our conversation was spectacular. I learned that the two were aunt and niece. The aunt was a lawyer at a prominent law firm across the bay in Kowloon. Her niece was interning at her firm throughout the summer. Toward the end of our meal, I dropped by the restroom only to return to the table cleaned off and occupied by new people. My friends were gone.

After finishing your meal, it is customary to bring your bill to the counter near the door, pay it, and leave; however, this becomes much more difficult when you can't find it. So, I frantically scoured my pockets, tore through every corner of my backpack, and asked the new group at our table if they had seen it.

The bill had vanished.

Confused and embarrassed, I walked to the counter and explained my situation to the cashier. She assured me that I was free to go because two ladies at my table paid for my lunch. I walked outside quickly to see if I could thank them, but they were long gone by then.

Another "Godwink."

My last few days in Hong Kong quickly approached. I refused to waste them.

If you know me, you'll know my love for travel guides. I buy the DK Eyewitness guide for every destination I plan to visit and thoroughly read it before traveling. The books weigh me down, but I bring all of them on the trip with me anyway. To lighten the load and pay it forward, I leave each book at the Airbnb or hotel I stay in as a gift to fellow travelers coming behind me.

After reading through the Hong Kong travel guide, I identified the Big Buddha statue in Lantau as a must-see highlight to visit. The weather looked suitable for the day, so I set off on my adventure. To get to the statue, I rode the Ngong Ping 360 cable car. This gondola ride lasted 25 minutes and presents a breathtaking view of Hong Kong from the sky. At the end of the line sits the base village near the statue. To get to the 112 ft Big Buddha statue at the top of the mountain, I climbed 268 steps up a beautiful stone staircase.

On the climb up, I passed hundreds of people taking pictures, stopping to rest, or climbing back down from the top.

About halfway up, I was abruptly stopped by a woman when she turned around and looked at me to shout in what sounded like an Australian accent, "Aye, you! Come over here! Look at this huge spider!" For most people (including myself), this statement belongs in a nightmare.

I hate spiders!

Overcoming my fear, I heeded her command and walked over to the edge of the staircase to set eyes on the most giant and most beautiful spider I have ever seen. Upon a quick Google search, I discovered what we were looking at was a Golden Orb Weaver spider. Its leg span is more than 6 inches wide: terrifying and amazing, dangerous and beautiful.

Looking around, we could point out more and more of these spiders in the woods that everyone else had passed by without regard. I would have passed it by, too, had it not been for this woman. She and I began to draw others' attention to the spiders, and within a few minutes, a small crowd had formed. After the spectacle concluded, she and I walked to the top of the stairs talking as we went.

On our walk up the stairs, the woman told me her name is Zöe. Zöe grew up on the North Island of New Zealand and worked as a marine biologist. She took a picture of me in front of the Buddha, and I returned the favor. At that point, we said a pleasant goodbye and moved on.

Or so I thought.

After a half-hour of exploring, I accidentally walked into the background of one of her photos. We reconnected and picked back up on our conversation where we had left off. She told me that she planned to walk down the "Wisdom Path" by the monastery. She asked if I cared to tag along. I had no plans for the rest of the afternoon, so I obliged. What we intended to be a short stroll turned into a 3-hour hike to one of the prettiest places I have ever seen. We talked about our families, friends, politics, similarities, differences, and faith along the trek. Zöe and I had many differences, but for every difference, there was a world of commonalities.

We walked back to the entrance of the compound to take the gondola back to town. Neither of us had eaten dinner yet, so we explored the alleyways of Hong Kong only to find some of the tastiest street food I've eaten to date. Finally, we took the MTR (metro/subway) to our respective stops, hugged, and said our final goodbye.

Or so I thought.

The following day, Zöe messaged me via WhatsApp to ask me if I would be interested in accompanying her to Lamma Island, a small island of fishing villages. I gladly accepted her invitation. First, we tried to catch a ferry to Yung Shue Wan, but we missed it by 20 minutes. The next ferry to that location would not be leaving for another half hour or so. Then, we noticed a ferry to a smaller village, Sok Kwu Wan, was sailing in ten minutes. So, spontaneously, we decided to take it.

We arrived at Sok Kwu Wan, explored for a bit, and sat down to one of the most memorable meals I've ever eaten. The restaurant was full of fish tanks. Instead of a menu, you simply point at a tasty-looking creature in the tanks. Then, minutes later, your waiter brings it to your table, fully cooked with all the fixings—a truly unique culinary experience.

Zoë asked if I wanted to take another stroll, but this time, down the "Lamma Island Family Walk," which connects the Sok Kwu Wan and Lamma Island fishing villages to one another. There were no automobiles on the island, so the walking trail is the main highway. We walked nearly four miles, stopping regularly to take in nature or to snap some pictures. We saw caves, natural springs, wildflowers, and beaches, among other things. Ironically, the last thing we spotted together happened to be the same type of spider that brought us together in the first place. This time,

I brought the spider to her attention instead of her drawing it to mine.

Zoë's flight departed late that night, so we left the island to our respective stops. Once again, we hugged and said our goodbyes, this time, indefinitely. We had grown so close in a matter of just 36 hours. We agreed that our trips would have been much different had we not met.

During our final conversation together, Zöe admitted she was supposed to visit Hong Kong two weeks prior, but due to circumstances out of her control, she pushed her trip back to the week I was in town. As you know by now, I was not supposed to arrive in Hong Kong until the following day.

Zoë and I should have never met. So many things and events had to occur for our paths to cross, and they all did.

I made a great friend in Zöe. I will never forget our adventures together. I know God put me in Hong Kong for a reason, and the primary reason was to share two incredible days of my life with a brilliant new friend.

Had either of our paths gone to plan, we would never have met. Yet, it was only by taking a detour that we formed a magical friendship, shared special days, and learned valuable lessons.

Jesus began his three-year ministry sometime between 26-29 AD at the age of thirty. In chapter 4 of John's Gospel, Jesus left Judea to visit Galilee. He and his disciples took an atypical route through Samaria. In Samaria, Jesus connected with a woman getting water from a well. It's important to note that although Samaritans and Israelites lived very close to one another geographically, they held very different worldviews. Significant cultural and religious differences led most Samaritans and Hebrews to dissociate from one another to the point of hatred.

We read in John's account that the woman was drawing water at an atypical time. Jesus sat by the well because he was tired from his journeys. Jesus asked the woman for a drink of water. She responded dumbfounded because this request was extremely countercultural to Jewish and Samaritan culture.

Rather than explain the interaction between the Samaritan woman and Jesus, I'll let you read John 4 for yourself. It is a beautiful picture of two people whose paths should have never crossed, but it made all the difference because they did.

Jesus intentionally went out of his way to meet the Samaritan woman. I didn't intentionally go out of my way to meet Zöe, and she didn't intentionally go out of her way to meet me either, but we both went out of our way, nonetheless. Jesus knew all there was to know about the Samaritan woman when he met her. Zöe and I knew little to nothing about each other when we met. Jesus is the perfect Son of God, and the Samaritan woman was ashamed and full of baggage. I am a follower of Jesus, but nothing close to excellent. Zöe is a successful, internationally renowned marine biologist with big dreams and a zest for life.

My story with Zoë looks vastly different from that of Jesus and the Samaritan woman. So too does the set and setting, characters, and context; however, what is the same is the magic that occurred because two people went out of their way, crossed each other's path, and neither of them let the opportunity pass by without making the most of it.

I have a new appreciation for the woman at the well and her story because of Zöe. I am thankful to serve a God who goes out of his way to meet us where we are and sends us out of our way to meet brothers and sisters whom he has appointed to be in our story and us in theirs.

F.A.V.O.R. DISCUSSION QUESTIONS
CHAPTER 4

Foundation: John 4:3-9 NIV "So he left Judea and went back once more to Galilee. Now he had to go through Samaria. So he came to a town in Samaria called Sychar, near the plot of ground Jacob had given to his son Joseph. Jacob's well was there, and Jesus, tired as he was from the journey, sat down by the well. It was about noon. When a Samaritan woman came to draw water, Jesus said to her, "Will you give me a drink?"

Application: How can you go out of your way for someone today?

Vision: In the future, how do you plan to connect with others different than you?

Orientation: To whom in your life is this story relevant? Write their name down and share it with them.

Name: _____

Reflection: Think back on your life. How does one of your experiences connect with Jesus and the Samaritan woman by the well?

5
the art of accepting an invitation

From Hong Kong, I flew to Tokyo, Japan, then to Bangkok, Thailand. I spent three days in each. Then, from Thailand, I flew to Bali, where our story begins.

I didn't have transportation of my own, so I spent most of my time near the capital city of Denpasar. Also, based on the driving I saw during my ride from the airport, I found myself unqualified to take on the bustling Balinese highways.

I met some incredible people on my walkabouts and got an excellent feel for Denpasar; however, the city isn't what I traveled to Bali to see. So, I ordered a rideshare and fled the city to the village of Ubud. The unofficial cultural capital of Bali, Ubud boasts a magnificent mosaic of Hindu temples, nature, food, and art.

After touring Ubud for the day, I rented a ride-share called "Grab" and headed back to my Airbnb in Denpasar. The driver, Hari, transported me while his three-year-old son sat in the front seat, fast asleep. Throughout our more than an hour-long car ride, Hari and I shared in one of the most profound and most meaningful spiritual conversations of my life.

At the end of the conversation, Hari asked me, "Would you like to spend tomorrow with my family and me?"

"I will drive you around the island wherever you want to go. My eldest son can be your translator. Honestly, I only drive for Grab to meet special people like you to share our island with more personally."

I was both flattered and taken back by his offer. Throughout my journeys thus far, I noticed it was semi-common practice for rideshare drivers to propose being your private transportation throughout your stay. Not only does private touring provide them with steady business, but they likely make more money in the end on tips. To this point, I had turned down every rideshare driver's request to be my personal transportation.

"Was Hari just another rideshare driver selling me on his services? I didn't know him very well, but he seemed different from the others. Hari felt safe, but most dangerous people do at first. If I go with him tomorrow, who knows where I'll end up? No guarantees. This guy could be lying to me to trick me." These thoughts and more raced through my head.

I quickly responded to Hari, "Let me sleep on it tonight. I'll text you tomorrow morning if I'm in. I appreciate the offer either way."

"No problem," said Hari, "I hope you will accept."

We exchanged contact information and went our separate ways.

That night, I didn't get much sleep. I spent most of the night racking my brain about all the things that could go wrong, and my anxiety level continued to rise. I finally fell asleep, with my answer being "no." But, surprisingly, I woke up with the answer being "yes."

And that "yes" made all of the difference.

I rolled out of bed and immediately texted Hari asking for directions to his house. I feared the invitation had expired. Thankfully, Hari held out for me.

I arrived in a small, residential neighborhood in Denpasar and walked inside Hari's home. The place was open-air, a bit damp from the humidity outside, and smelled of excellent food cooking in the kitchen. Five kids crowded around a television watching a multilingual educational children's program.

Hari greeted me with a smile and a giant hug. "Hello friend, sit and eat with me."

He introduced me to his children and began to fill my plate with various fruits and vegetables.

"We are vegetarians. I raised all of my children on vegetarian diets, and the entire community thought I was crazy. They told me that my children would be malnourished and underdeveloped if they didn't eat meat. Look at them now. They are beautiful, healthy, and top of their class in school. Now, my neighbors and their kids are vegetarians."

"Very impressive!" I said as I continued to scarf down my incredible breakfast spread.

"All of the fruits and vegetables you're eating right now are organically grown. They come from my fields on the northern part of the island. Aren't they wonderful?" Hari asked.

"They're incredible," I said as I peeled a banana the size of my forearm.

Hari didn't know my disdain for bananas, so I mustered up the courage to eat the whole thing, hoping he wouldn't notice. To my surprise, the banana was delicious and filling. Since that day, I have eaten more bananas than any other fruit.

"Where do you want to go today?" Hari asked.

"I don't have a preference," I answered. "I'd like to see the Tanah Lot Temple, if possible, but take me wherever you think is best. You're a local. I trust you."

Hari, his eldest son, and I packed up their family van and headed north. On our journey, we visited multiple temples and landmarks and even stopped by a couple of his farms periodically along the way to pick mangoes, bananas, and other tropical fruits.

Hari would also occasionally pull over on the side of the road to buy me local street food to try. Jackfruit, pastries, and other delicacies filled my stomach with painful joy.

"Have you ever heard of Luwak coffee?" Hari asked.

"Never," I said nervously. I doubted I had any room left in my stomach.

Hari handed his iPhone to me to show me an episode of a show called "Most Expensivest" where the host, Atlanta rapper 2 Chainz, discussed Luwak coffee. Luwak coffee is the most expensive coffee in the world. The video explains that the civet is a nocturnal mammal whose diet consists of coffee fruit. After digesting the fruit, the civet expels coffee beans in its excrement. "Hold on a second," I said, "so you're telling me that an animal eats the coffee, poops the coffee, and then we drink the coffee?" I asked, puzzled and a bit disgusted. "Exactly. It's the finest coffee in the world. Just wait and see."

Hari turned off the main road and into the Luwak coffee plantation. Civets kept on-site were brought out and allowed to crawl on our shoulders as we sampled various brews of their work.

This is going to be an expensive little outing. I thought as I remembered 2 Chainz's episode, I'm drinking the most expensive coffee in the world, and a lot of it!

As we exited through their version of a gift shop, I asked Hari how much I owed for my coffee tour.

"Nothing," said Hari, "my family owns the plantation."

Stunned, I thanked and tipped the staff for their hospitality, and we headed to the final stop of the day, Garuda Wisnu Kencana Cultural Park. We took pictures next to some of the world's largest statues before heading to the airport for departure. It was around 8:30 PM. The sun was setting on my last day in Bali.

"I cannot thank you enough for today," I said to Hari.

"You're very welcome, my friend. It is our pleasure to have you on our island."

I asked Hari how much I owed for his services for the day.

"Pay me whatever you think today was worth. If it was worth nothing to you, pay me nothing. If it was worth a lot to you, pay me a lot. I will be content either way."

I gave Hari all the cash in my wallet. It totaled around $80. Hari embraced me and said, "Thank you, brother. When you come back to Bali, you stay with my family, and you eat with my family. You are part of our family now. I love you and hope to see you soon, my brother."

While waiting on my flight to Sydney, which departed at 11:00 PM, I decided to get a bite of dinner in the main concourse. I met a British girl and invited her to sit with me. She had been in Bali for the past two and a half months, and she was returning to London. Toward the end of our hour-long conversation, I stood up to leave for security check-in.

Looking through emails for my boarding pass, I began to laugh.

"What is it?" she said.

"Seems as though my flight took off last night," I replied.

Since my flight to Australia was overnight, I had mistaken the dates of departure and arrival. "It's okay,"

I told her, "Things like this happen to me all the time. It will all work out as it needs to."

She was stunned. "You're crazy. I would be freaking out," she replied.

I was reminded of my run-in with God in Toronto the week before. I knew he was in control now more than ever. I walked up to the check-in desk, just as I did in Toronto. I told the desk agent my situation, just as I did in Toronto. She booked me the last remaining seat, the very same seat, on the next flight out, just as they did in Toronto.

Although my time in Australia would now be one day shorter, my extra day in Bali proved to be more valuable and memorable than I ever imagined.

Thank God I said "Yes."

In the Gospels of Matthew, Mark, and Luke, we see three separate yet beautiful accounts of one miraculous invitation to unsuspecting men. But, while Matthew and Mark cover the story, Luke truly illustrates it for us in chapter 5 of his gospel. Because of Jesus's teaching, a crowd has formed around him near the Sea of Galilee, or as Luke calls it, the "Lake of Gennesaret."

A professional fisherman named Simon (also referred to as Peter in later chapters) and his brother Andrew have been fishing to no avail. So, Jesus stepped onto their boat and asked them to let out into the water a bit. Then, Jesus began to preach a message from the ship to the crowd on the shore.

Jesus then asked the brothers to put out to deeper water and let their nets down for a catch.

This request seemed unreasonable to Simon, who, in true Simon fashion, makes sure to let Jesus know that the brothers have not caught a single fish all night.

Also, in true Simon fashion, he eventually obeyed Jesus's request saying, "But, because you say so, I will let down the nets." Luke 5:5 NIV

To their pleasant surprise, Simon and Andrew's net was filled with fish. So much so that as they attempt to bring the catch into the boat, the ship begins to sink. Simon immediately repents his sin, knowing that the man in his midst must be of divine origin. Simon and Andrew's fishing partners, another set of brothers, James and John, are also recorded to have had a similar reaction to Jesus's miracle catch.

While not found in Luke, Matthew and Mark record Jesus's ultimate invitation to these four ordinary men. "Come, follow me. And I will make you fishers of men." Matt 4:19 NIV

All four dropped everything they were doing and followed Jesus.

Doesn't it amaze you how much a single invitation can impact a life? Of course, it's human to worry and be anxious when accepting an invitation from a total stranger. But do you think Simon, Andrew, James, and John blindly accepted the invitation and followed Jesus without concern? No way! They had their doubts and reservations too.

But then they received a front-row seat for watching Jesus perform miracle to miracle, healing to healing, and victory to victory as he cast out demons, made the blind see, and died for the sins of the world. Do you think they still had doubts and reservations after seeing Jesus beaten and crucified for them? Nope.

How do I know? Because all four of these men and many others died similar, heinous deaths as Jesus to share the message of hope he brought to the world.

I have no doubt these four great disciples looked back on their lives before their death. I picture them laughing at the concern that felt so real on that day at the lake, now wondering what there was to be afraid of in the first place. I know I sure did after my day on the island with Hari.

Was my day in Bali anywhere close to the miraculous ministry of the Son of God or his disciples? No. But, when I look back on a miraculous day of my own with a man who offered me a simple invitation to trust and follow his lead, I only see the similarity between these disciples and me.

We all had other places to be.

Simon and Andrew should have gone home after a failed day on the sea. I should have been on a flight to Australia. But because neither these men nor I were where we were "supposed" to be, we were able to accept an invitation that we could have never imagined being given by a man we never "should" have met because of a simple invitation to drop our plans at the door and follow someone we barely know into the unknown.

Our "yes" made all the difference.

F.A.V.O.R. DISCUSSION QUESTIONS
CHAPTER 5

Foundation: Matthew 4:18-22 NIV "As Jesus was walking beside the Sea of Galilee, he saw two brothers, Simon called Peter and his brother Andrew. They were casting a net into the lake, for they were fishermen. "Come, follow me," Jesus said, "and I will send you out to fish for people." At once they left their nets and followed him. Going on from there, he saw two other brothers, James son of Zebedee and his brother John. They were in a boat with their father Zebedee, preparing their nets. Jesus called them, and immediately they left the boat and their father and followed him."

Application: How might you be called into the unknown today?

Vision: When someone invites you to step out of your comfort zone in the future, how can you ease your fear of the unknown?

Orientation: To whom in your life is this story relevant? Write their name down and share it with them.

Name: _____

Reflection: Think back on your life. How does one of your experiences connect with Simon and Andrew?

6
the art of quitting your job

Over 36 days, I had visited Hong Kong, Tokyo, Bangkok, Bali, Sydney and ended in New Zealand. The journey was incredible, but I had to come home eventually.

A few months before leaving for Asia, I had accepted a sales position at a startup lighting company in the Atlanta suburb of Alpharetta. In addition, I moved all my belongings to Georgia the week before leaving on my trip.

While in Tokyo, I got a phone call from the national sales director at the lighting company, Trevor, with the news that my position had been reconsidered and terminated. The news bummed me out, but who cares? I was on the most impactful trip of my life. I couldn't afford to let my future job in Atlanta negatively affect my present experience in Asia. God had me covered; I knew it.

Thankfully, I had not signed a lease on an apartment yet. Family friends on Lake Lanier allowed me to live with them until Thanksgiving. I returned to the United States around Labor Day in September. I began the job search upon my arrival.

I applied for various positions throughout the next few weeks. Unfortunately, each application was either denied or met with silence. It was easy to get down on myself after a while.

Later in the week, I received some much-needed good news in the form of a text from a previous co-worker at the company I interned with in college.

"Hamilton, it's Stephen. Give me a call when you can. I heard you were looking for a job in Atlanta. Dewey has a meeting set up for you."

I immediately picked up the phone and called him. Later that week, Dewey, the company owner, connected me to a friend of his in Buckhead named Bill. Bill is co-founder and managing partner of a leading hospitality real estate transaction firm. After doing some research, I concluded that this opportunity was a BIG deal. Bill's firm handled billions in transactions each year and maintained a high level of respect in the hospitality industry. I felt honored that Dewey thought highly enough of me to make the introduction.

I scheduled an interview with Bill for Tuesday of the following week. On Sunday evening, leading up to my meeting with Bill, Trevor called me from the lighting company.

"Hey man, it's Trevor. I know this sounds weird, but I think we might have a spot open for you again at the lighting company. We took on a pretty large account, and now we need someone to handle most of my older accounts. Are you still interested? If not, I understand."

I told Trevor I was entertaining other offers at the time, but I was still open to an opportunity at the lighting company. My interview with Bill wasn't until Tuesday, so I spent Monday shadowing Trevor and the team. On my way out the door, Trevor handed me an offer letter valid until the end of the week. I told Trevor about my interview with Bill and explained that I would most likely take it if an opportunity arose with Bill's firm. Trevor understood.

The next day, I met Bill on the 17th floor of Buckhead's tallest skyrise. I expected the meeting to last no more than thirty minutes. Instead, Bill and I connected and talked for two hours. Bill and I discovered that we were both Jesus followers and brothers of the same college fraternity. Everything just seemed to click.

By the end of the meeting, Bill offered to create a position for me. I was honored. I thanked Bill for this opportunity and told him about the competing opportunity at the lighting company. I had a big decision to make, and I'd need some time to think and pray about it. Bill understood.

That night reminded me a lot of the night Hari invited me to spend the following day with him in Bali. I was restless, anxious, and my head raced all night. I prayed to God, asking for guidance on my decision. I planned to go into the lighting company Wednesday morning to either accept or deny the offer.

On my way to the office, I still had not made my decision. Finally, I began to pray out loud in the car. "Lord, please give me an answer as to what You would have me do. Show me your path for my life." At that very moment, my phone began to ring.

"Good morning, Hamilton. It's Bill. I've been thinking and praying a lot about your decision, and I trust you have as well. I don't know what you have decided, but I wanted to call you before getting to the lighting company. I think you should give them a try before coming on board with us. The position sounds like a great entry-level opportunity for you. If you don't like it after a year or so, call me, and we'll hire you here. What do you say?"

I was instantly at peace. God had immediately answered my prayer.

"Thank you for calling, Bill. I think you're right. This call was an answered prayer. I appreciate all you've done for me so far. Talk soon."

I walked into the lighting company office and signed the offer letter. I was officially employed. I held the title of senior sales representative. They gave me a credit card, an expense account, and free reign. We played corn hole at the office in the afternoons and got drunk every Thursday at a Mexican restaurant down the street from the office. On paper, I had the perfect job for a 22-year-old.

In reality, that job and that year would prove to be the most difficult, trying, and darkest time in my life to that point. With no formal training or guidance, I was all but thrown to the wolves. A good day meant I didn't get chastised or chased out of an office for simply doing my job.

Winter arrived much colder than I expected in more ways than one. I went on dates, but no deep relationships formed. I made some friends, but most of them moved or fell away over time. I felt alone and empty.

A childhood friend from Louisiana, Kaitlyn, had moved to Atlanta a couple of years before me. Kaitlyn called me one day and invited me to come to church with her. She spoke very highly of the pastor and worship music. So, I agreed to accompany her. I hadn't been to church in a while.

On a cold Sunday in December 2017, I walked into Passion City Church. Volunteers greeted Kaitlyn and me with a smile as soon as we walked through the door. Their attention to detail and intentionality struck me. Worship proved to be even better than Kaitlyn described.

As soon as I asked myself could it get any better, the pastor took the stage. I recognized his face immediately. Nearly a decade ago, a random video popped up on my Facebook page. The video contained a sermon about the magnitude of our solar system and a miracle molecule within the human body called "laminin." The presentation blew my mind, and I never forgot about it.

Louie Giglio preached that sermon. Ten years later, I find myself walking blindly into my neighborhood church only to realize Louie is the pastor of Passion City Church.

I felt at home.

Church proved to be the only positive light during that season of my life. As winter turned into spring, each day seemed to call out louder than the day before,

"You're meant for more, Hamilton. You're meant for more."

While driving around Atlanta prospecting for sales, I blared music on full volume in the car. That voice in my head sounded so loud that I could barely hear the music at all.

I knew I had a purpose, but that purpose evaded me. Growing up in church as a child, I heard stories of people returning to faith and discovering their calling. I hadn't read the Bible much to that point, but the present seemed as good a time as ever to start.

I began to dive into the Word each day. I also began praying out loud when I woke up and before I went to sleep. Short devotionals quickly graduated to longer, more in-depth studies of the Scripture. I couldn't seem to get enough. I joined a community group through Passion City and applied to become a volunteer at the church. I could finally see the light at the end of the tunnel.

In March, I decided I needed to confront the elephant in the room. I hated my job, but I refused to quit. I wanted to give the lighting company at least a full year, but I needed to find something to take my mind off of my job in the meantime.

One of my friends had recently recommended I write my life goals down on paper. I had the afternoon to myself, so I took his advice. On the very top of my list sat "learn to fly."

Nothing ever fascinated me quite like airplanes. Every time I saw one, I transformed back into my three-year-old self, full of wonder and glee. On my drives around Atlanta, I noticed a small, private airport home to several flight schools near my apartment. With my flexible work schedule, I could take flight lessons part-time. Bingo. I think I found my distraction.

I called a few flight schools at Dekalb-Peachtree Airport to see what was available. Unfortunately, a few schools either didn't answer or told me they weren't taking on new students at the time. So, I decided to make one final call.

A man with a harsh New York accent answered the phone. His language was vulgar, offensive, and rude. I considered hanging up on him, but I decided to be the bigger man. Toward the end of the phone call, he dropped the act and admitted his behavior was a screening tactic for prospective students. He invited me to tour the flight school, and if I was interested, to register for classes the following Monday.

I immediately began doing my research on pilot training. On Monday, I arrived at the airport a bit early to watch airplanes take off and land. I was beyond inspired. I walked into the flight school, registered, and began taking classes that week. It was the week of my birthday, March 29.

I flew three to four times a week. Not only did I love flying, but I proved to be quite good at it, too. After four months of training, I earned my private pilot certificate in a record 42 hours of flight time. Had I found my calling? I thought so. I wrestled hard with the decision to quit my job and train full-time.

I had always dreamed of becoming a professional aviator. Given the global pilot shortage, demand for airline pilots had recently skyrocketed. I would finally be able to do what I have always wanted to do, and I would be paid for it. Best of all, I wouldn't have to work at the lighting company anymore.

Only one problem, while I earned all of my certifications, I would be spending money rather than making it. This decision would be a significant financial setback for me and would require a great deal of time. But this was my shot. God had answered my prayers.

If I didn't jump, I would regret it for the rest of my life.

I called Trevor at the lighting company and told him my plans. I put in my notice, and two weeks later, I became a full-time student again. Was I crazy? Only time would tell.

One of Jesus's disciples, Matthew, was a tax collector. On paper, tax collecting was one of the best careers in the ancient world. Benefits included steady income, the opportunity to line one's own pockets by charging excess fees, and the support of the Roman Empire. However, citizens of Capernaum, his parents included, despised him.

Tax collectors were known as cheats and thieves—the sinners of sinners. Matthew was a self-professed tax collector and a good one at that. One day a man from Galilee came along and made him a disciple.

"As Jesus went on from there, he saw a man named Matthew sitting at the tax collector's booth. 'Follow me,' he told him, and Matthew got up and followed him." Matthew 9:9 NIV

What Jesus didn't ask but instead implied was, "Quit your job...and follow me." Without hesitation, Matthew quit his job and followed Jesus.

The hesitation might not be apparent, but the risk sure is. Matthew stepped away from financial and personal security, a steady job, and the comforts afforded to him by Rome and the money he stole. Was the job miserable? Probably. But was that a logical reason to step away in this day in age? No. It wouldn't make any sense.

But a call to something greater taunted Matthew and me when the opportunity knocked to quit our jobs. What awaited us was an adventure that required risk but held a much greater reward, and a chance to use our talents and be fulfilled instead of being forced to choose between the two.

Matthew, the tax collector, quit his job to follow the Son of God on his tour to save the world. Hamilton, the senior sales representative, quit his job to take flight school lessons and accomplish a dream to fly. We are on many different scales than one another, yet the premise is the same. As my dad always says, "Nothing happens when you do nothing."

Calling requires action. Action involves risk. Risk begets reward.

Take the plunge. The water might be cold, but the experience is unmatched. You either jump or spend the rest of your life regretting and justifying why you didn't.

F.A.V.O.R. DISCUSSION QUESTIONS
CHAPTER 6

Foundation: Matthew 9:9 NIV "As Jesus went on from there, he saw a man named Matthew sitting at the tax collector's booth. 'Follow me,' he told him, and Matthew got up and followed him."

Application: If Jesus asked you to quit your job today, could you? Would you? Should you?

Vision: What calling do you see God placing on your life in the future?

Orientation: To whom in your life is this story relevant? Share it with them.

Name: _____

Reflection: Think back on your life. How does one of your experiences connect with Matthew?

7
the art of ordering food

I enjoyed Asia so much on the first trip that I decided to go back a year later! My favorite music group, Above & Beyond, scheduled a hallmark show in Hong Kong. Since my last visit, I yearned to return. I planned my 2018 trip to be half as long as my 2017 trip. I would travel eighteen days instead of thirty-six, hitting four stops instead of six. Since I couldn't get to China in 2017, I decided to give it another shot. So, I stuffed my backpack and flew to Shanghai. From Shanghai, I caught a flight to the towering city of Kuala Lumpur, Malaysia! Malaysia was not on my initial itinerary; however, a layover in Kuala Lumpur made the flight from Shanghai to Singapore significantly less expensive than direct.

I'll admit, I spent a great deal of my time in Kuala Lumpur at our hotel's rooftop infinity pool overlooking the skyline. Not a bad layover, I thought to myself as I watched a couple of Russian Instagram models taking selfies by the pool.

I brought my dirty laundry from Shanghai, intending to wash it in Kuala Lumpur. So, I found a laundromat near my hotel. After dropping my hamper off at the cleaners, I went back to my room to determine where to eat for the night. I soon realized all my recently converted Malaysian Ringgits were inside the pocket of a pair of shorts now at the laundromat.

I rushed down to get the shorts only to see a sign with big, red letters on the door reading "CLOSED." I would have to wait until morning. I had no food, no water, and no ATM existed anywhere near me.

Way to go, Hamilton.

With an empty stomach and one relatively clean set of clothes to wear, I decided to just go to sleep.

The following day, I walked a few blocks over to a shopping mall to find an ATM. To my disappointment, the mall was not open for another two hours. I walked toward a security guard outside the entrance and told him my situation. I explained my only intention was to visit the ATM and asked if he could help me. He reluctantly unlocked the front door of the mall and escorted me inside to withdraw some cash. On our way to the ATM, I noticed a very lovely food court inside. I decided the food court would be where I ate lunch that day. Having not eaten dinner the night before, I daydreamed about my new lunch plans. I thanked the guard and went directly to a convenience store for water and a snack.

As soon as the clock struck 11:00 AM, I returned to the food court of the mall. Doing a quick flyby of the multitude of restaurants inside, I caught a glimpse of three Swedish girls I met earlier at the pool. They sat inside of one of the restaurants I considered eating in.

Never shy of a challenge, I debated whether or not to walk in and sit down with them. After a few moments of discernment, I determined pretty girls were not on the agenda for this trip, but good food was. After looking over the menus of a few restaurants and seeing various tasty options, I chose the restaurant next to where the girls were eating. The place I decided on was called "Chicken Rice Shop."

I was seated at a table by myself along the front of the restaurant. A woman and her son sat at the only other table occupied in my section. The waiter came over to take my order.

I ordered two roasted chicken breasts and some steamed vegetables with sauce. After reviewing my choices, the waiter asked me, "Would you like rice with that, sir?"

"No, thank you," I replied.

Confused and a bit startled, the waiter asked, "No? But sir, the rice is delicious."

"No, thank you," I said, "I am trying to cut down on carbs, so I'll stick with just the chicken and veggies, please."

"As you wish, sir." He walked away, puzzled. I was puzzled too.

Why would he even ask the question if the only acceptable answer was "Yes?" Whatever, I shrugged it off and went back to scrolling through my Instagram feed.

A few moments later, the lady with her son at the nearby table motioned to me.

"Your waiter doesn't speak English very well. He was a bit confused thinking you don't want the rice," she said.

"That's correct. I don't want the rice. I'm on a low-carb diet," I said, clarifying my position.

"You didn't want the rice? But it's excellent here. You should try it!"

"Okay, thank you. I'll consider it," I said.

I thought to myself, "I usually eat in peace. So, what's up with everyone wanting me to try this stupid rice?"

Just then, I see the restaurant manager walk up to the lady and begin to speak with her in Malay. Judging by their body language, they were talking about me.

The manager then walks over to me and says, "Hello sir, are you enjoying everything so far?"

"Yes. Everything is great, thank you." I replied.

"Sir, I heard you didn't order the rice with your meal. Is this true?"

"That's correct," I said.

"Well, sir, the rice is what we are known for here at Chicken Rice Shop. You should try it."

A bit frustrated at this point, I explained my low-carb diet for the final time.

"I understand, sir. But, if I ordered you some rice and paid for it myself, would you try it?" the manager asked.

"Yes, of course," I responded, not wanting to offend.

It seems as though I'm going to have to eat this rice one way or another. The waiter immediately brought an enormous bowl of rice to my table, and I tried it as promised.

I won't lie. The rice was excellent; however, it didn't change the fact that I didn't usually eat rice. But if I did, this rice would be the rice I would choose to eat.

The manager introduced himself as Zaidi, sat down at my table, and began to ask me about my trip. Right off the bat, Zaidi reminded me of my Balinese friend, Hari, from chapter 5. Both had a kind-hearted demeanor and sincere smile reinforced with a gentle but sure tone of voice. As we learned more about each other, Zaidi continued to summon the waiter to bring me more food and drinks to try.

I'm nearly positive I tried every item on their menu.

Zaidi and I became close friends over lunch. We shared stories about each other's family, past experiences, exotic travels, all while amassing a table full of entrees, teas, coffees, desserts, and drinks.

I planned to visit a few attractions that afternoon, so I would need to leave relatively soon to fit everything in. I didn't want to leave Zaidi, but it was time to say goodbye.

Or so I thought.

"I can't thank you enough, my friend," I said, looking down at the table. I felt disgustingly full but satisfied.

"How much longer are you in Malaysia?" Zaidi asked.

"I leave tomorrow afternoon," I replied.

"Are there any things here in Kuala Lumpur that you would like to see?" Zaidi asked.

"I'd like to visit a few spots this afternoon, but nothing set in stone."

Zaidi looked down at his watch and said, "You're not like my other customers. There is something special about you, and I don't know what it is. What would you say if I was your private tour guide today? I can take off work in the next half hour, and I am free until I pick up my wife at five o'clock this afternoon. Then, I can show you the best parts of our city."

Thinking back to my incredible experience with Hari in Bali, I jumped at the opportunity.

"I would love to, but I don't want to infringe on your day," I said.

"Not at all. It would be my pleasure. Let me call my wife to see if it's okay with her," Zaidi said as he walked away to take the call.

A few minutes later, Zaidi returned to my table.

"Alright, we got the green light," Zaidi said. "Grab your stuff and follow me to my car. I park in the employee garage behind the mall."

"No problem. Let me pay my bill first, and then I'll be on my way," I replied.

"No need. I took care of it for you. You're my guest," Zaidi said.

"No, no," I replied. "I had so much of everything. Please at least let me pay for some of it."

"Not at all," Zaidi said. "I manage over fifty locations of this restaurant chain, so a complimentary meal for my new friend will not hurt our bottom line."

I thanked him, picked up my backpack, and we walked to the employee parking garage. After that, Zaidi took me all over the city to spots I never knew existed. As Hari had done, Zaidi and I would occasionally pull over to sample local delicacies from street food vendors. I was as stuffed as I could remember, but I kept eating so as not to offend.

As we were driving, Zaidi's phone rang. It was his wife.

"Hamilton, I need to pick my wife up. She is getting her automobile serviced. Would you like to meet her?" Zaidi asked.

"Of course! I'd be delighted," I said.

Making a U-turn, we swung by the auto body shop to pick up Kamaridah, Zaidi's wife.

Kamaridah was a beautiful woman dressed nicely in a decorative hijab on her head.

From the back of the car, she said, "My husband is quite fond of you. He rarely speaks of his guests and never brings them to meet us." I was flattered.

She went on, "He also doesn't spend much time at the location you visited. He wasn't even supposed to work there today. So, it seems as though luck was in both of your favor."

No coincidences.

The couple and I visited a few more tourist spots as the afternoon drew to a close. Five PM was our agreed-upon cut-off time, so it was nearly time to say goodbye.

Or so I thought.

As we passed a row of commercial buildings, Zaidi spoke up.

"The restaurant to your left is my favorite place to eat in all of Kuala Lumpur," he said. "Hamilton, have you ever eaten with your hands?" "Never," I replied.

He immediately pulled the car into a space in front of the restaurant, and we got out to eat our third full meal of the afternoon. Zaidi and Kamaridah taught me how to eat Indian curry with my hands. We shared a culinary experience I will never forget.

I still don't know how I had room in my stomach for all that food. But honestly, I'd rather not think about it.

"Are you in a hurry for us to take you back to your hotel?" Zaidi asked.

"No. But I'm happy to go back whenever I need to. I don't want to wear out my welcome," I answered. "Hamilton, I would like for you to visit my home and meet my children. Would you like to do that? They would love to meet you."

"I would be honored," I said as Zaidi re-routed the car toward his home.

We spent the evening talking, laughing, and playing in their humble but cozy Malaysian flat. We drank instant Nescafe, ate local snacks, and shared beautiful moments of life. It was a night I will never forget.

In total, Zaidi and I spent more than eight hours together. What a day.

After realizing we had far surpassed the kids' bedtime, the family and I loaded up the car and headed toward the hotel. As we neared my destination, the car continued past my drop-off point.

"That's my hotel back there," I politely reminded Zaidi.

Kamaridah answered me, saying, "He knows. Zaidi just wanted to spend an extra moment or two with you."

She turned toward Zaidi and said, "Come on, honey, you know you have to drop him off."

Trying to hold back the tears, one slipped from my eye. I didn't want the day to end either.

When we pulled up to the hotel, Zaidi got out of the car and hugged me. He looked me in the eyes, gripped my hand, and said, "You are part of our family now. When you come back to Kuala Lumpur, you and your guests stay and eat with my family and me. We will never forget you. You are very special, and although we haven't known you for very long, it feels as though we have been friends forever.

Much love to you, my brother. Safe travels."

Zaidi then opened the back door of the car, motioning to his children to get out. "Kids, give big brother a hug." The family gathered around me to wish me goodbye. Then, they loaded up once more, and I watched the kids wave from the back window as the car drove away in the distance.

This time, I let the tears roll.

In the Old Testament, we learn of a man named Daniel. Around ~605 BC, Daniel and the Israelites living in the northern kingdom of Judah found themselves exiled, living amongst their conquerors, the Babylonians.

The first order of business for the King of Babylon, Nebuchadnezzar, was to set apart "...Israelites from the royal family and nobility without physical defect, handsome, showing aptitude for every kind of learning, well informed, quick to understand, and qualified to serve in the King's palace." Daniel 1:3 NIV

Daniel and his three friends, Hananiah, Mishael, and Azariah, were among the men chosen to serve the king. As was the custom of the day, captives received new names and were required to learn and use the language and literature of their captors. Changing their names served to psychologically erase their Jewish identity in replacement of a new, Babylonian identity. Thus, Daniel became "Belteshazzar," Hananiah became "Shadrach," Mishael became "Meshach," and Azariah became "Abednego."

After receiving their new identities, this group of men trained for three years, and each day received a daily amount of choice food and wine from the king's table. While this seemed like a decent proposal to most men, Daniel asked the chief official's permission not to defile himself under Jewish law by consuming the royal food and wine.

God caused the official to show favor and compassion to Daniel; however, the official worried about angering the king if, under his supervision, Daniel and his friends looked malnourished and underfed compared to the men eating from the king's table. Therefore, Daniel suggested the official test them for ten days feeding them only vegetables instead of choice food and wine.

After ten days, Daniel and his friends were visibly healthier and more well-nourished than their peers eating from the royal table. God blessed Daniel and his friends' decision by giving them knowledge and understanding of all kinds of literature and learning. To Daniel, God gives the gift of understanding visions and dreams.

When the chief official presented the Israelite men to Nebuchadnezzar, the king found none as healthy or strong as Daniel and his friends. In every matter of wisdom and understanding about which the king questioned them, King Nebuchadnezzar found Daniel, Shadrach, Meshach, and Abednego ten times better than all the magicians and enchanters in his whole kingdom.

Later in his story, Daniel uses God's gift of wisdom and prophecy to become one of the most well-known and respected prophets of all time. But for now, let's focus solely on chapter one of Daniel's story. Daniel's decision not to eat the traditional food was countercultural but blessed by God. Daniel and his friends had much more at stake when deciding not to eat the traditional food in Babylon than I had not to eat the traditional food in Malaysia. They risked defiling their bodies according to God's law. I risked putting on a few extra pounds. Either way, how or why you distinguish yourself pales in comparison to what you do with that distinction.

Had Daniel and his friends chosen to eat from the king's table as the rest of the group did, they would have missed an opportunity to rise in the ranks of the king's service and ultimately use it for God's glory. Likewise, had I done what everyone else did by ordering the rice, the restaurant manager would have had no reason to come to my table and strike up a conversation with me.

Daniel and his friends earned the king's favor. I made a friend I'll cherish forever.

God gives us many opportunities to distinguish ourselves. Sometimes opportunities present themselves in obvious ways. For example, at the office, we can distinguish ourselves by the quality of our work. At school, we can distinguish ourselves with high grades or extracurricular activities. In society, we can distinguish ourselves through service to the community, philanthropy, or involvement in local affairs.

Other opportunities conceal themselves. In some scenarios, we distinguish ourselves not by what we say, but rather by what we choose not to say. In other scenarios, we can distinguish ourselves not by what we do, but rather by what we choose not to do. Again, how or why you distinguish yourself pales in comparison to what you do with that distinction to further God's mission.

You might be thinking, "I get that you distinguished yourself by not ordering the rice, but how did you further God's mission?" I didn't know at first.

Upon arriving back in the United States after my trip, I reflected on this very question. Zaidi and his family practice Islam. Because we became friends in real life, Zaidi, his family, and I also became friends on Facebook. Most of my posts are about Jesus. Zaidi and his family see and react to nearly every one of them with either a like or love.

Who knows what impact our social media friendship is having on their hearts toward a relationship with Jesus? As believers, it is our job to sow the seeds of truth and love in the hearts of those around us. It's the Holy Spirit's job to cultivate that seed so we might be able to reap the harvest.

The moral of the story... watch what you eat.

F.A.V.O.R. DISCUSSION QUESTIONS
CHAPTER 7

Foundation: Daniel 6:3 NIV "Now Daniel so distinguished himself among the administrators and the satraps by his exceptional qualities that the king planned to set him over the whole kingdom."

Application: How are you distinguishing yourself like Daniel today?

Vision: When distinguished in the future, how will you use it to further God's mission?

Orientation: To whom in your life is this story relevant? Write their name down and share it with them.

Name: _____

Reflection: Think back on your life. How does one of your experiences connect with Daniel?

8

the art of going to class

After Malaysia, I spent a few days in Singapore before revisiting the magical city of Hong Kong for the Above & Beyond concert. I met some incredible friends along the way and experienced things that served as a catalyst and springboard for the rest of my life. More to come on this in another book.

This story came to fruition after returning home from my second Asian tour, but it started before I left. In spring 2018, a few short weeks into my flight school training, I completed my pre-flight inspections of the plane before takeoff. The flight school manager, Russell, approached me on the ramp and asked me to visit with him in his office inside the hangar. I walked into the office not knowing what the meeting was about, but I assumed I was in some sort of trouble.

"Hey man, I hope you're enjoying flying. You're doing well so far." Russell said in an encouraging and positive tone.

"Whew. I'm not in trouble" I thought to myself.

He continued, "I've been working at this school for a couple of years now. I feel I know it like the back of my hand by this point. I have an idea for a flight school concept that would change the aviation industry. I can't do it here, so, I'll have to start my own school. I've been looking for someone with a business and marketing background, and you just randomly showed up with a marketing degree and an MBA. Crazy! Anyway, would you like to hear the idea?" He had my attention. I agreed to hear him out.

By the end of the meeting, Russell and I had become business partners. I had no idea what this meant at the time, but I knew Russell believed in my business skills, and I believed in his vision to start a holistic and inviting flight training academy.

That afternoon I took to the drawing boards and came up with our company name, NSPIRE Aviation.

Unfortunately, going into business means more than creating a brand and having a good idea. Losing sight of the end goal is easy, especially if another goal competes with it. For me, building the business became a competing goal with my professional aviation career.

To become a major American airline pilot, you must complete all certifications and earn a minimum of 1500 flight hours. There are two main ways pilots typically make their hours:

Become a certified flight instructor (CFI) and teach others how to fly.

Knowing that my patience level is not as high as required for this job, I never seriously considered this option.

Enlist in the military as a pilot.

I had always dreamed of being a fighter pilot. This option not only made sense, but it excited me. I was twenty-three years old and in the best shape of my life. Without Russell knowing, I began researching and applying for the Air Force Reserves while building NSPIRE with Russell and training toward my private pilot certificate.

Over the summer, I connected with a recruiter from the Air Force. He assisted me in filling out all my paperwork in time for me to leave for Asia. I submitted all my forms the day I flew to Shanghai. Eighteen days abroad should be plenty of time for the paperwork to go through. He convinced me I was a shoo-in.

When I returned from Asia in October 2018, I knew I had to come clean to Russell. He deserved to know I was joining the Air Force, thus giving up on our business endeavor. Although the conversation would be challenging, it needed to happen.

Russell met me at PDK airport the day after I returned. I opened my mouth to tell him the unfortunate news, but before I could speak, Russell stopped me.

"Before you say anything, just follow me," Russell said. "I have a surprise for you."

I followed Russell into an area of the building I had never seen before. There were four office spaces down a hallway with beautiful glass windows.

"So, what do you think?" Russell asked.

"It's great! But what is it?" I responded, a bit confused.

"It's NSPIRE's new office. I got it for us while you were gone. Come let me show you what all I've been doing while you were gone."

I was speechless. I sat and listened as Russell told me the story about how he negotiated an incredible deal for the office spaces and revolutionized our entire business model. Russell was going all-in for me.

But I had other obligations to fulfill.

How was I supposed to tell Russell about the Air Force now!?

I was genuinely excited about all Russell had done while I was gone. After talking with him that day, I could finally see the why behind what we were working so hard to accomplish. It reinvigorated my passion, but was it too late?

Just before I fell asleep that night, an email from my Air Force Recruiter dropped into my inbox. The subject line said, "Action needed: signature missing." My heart dropped.

The recruiter informed me that he could not process my application in the email because I accidentally missed a signature line when filling out the forms.

The following day, I called the recruiter to tell him that I was pressing pause on my application. Rather than feeling disappointed or frustrated about the situation, I felt relieved. Was this God's hand guiding me? I prayed about it and received an overwhelming sense of peace in return.

I had other obligations to fulfill.

I met Russell at the office the next day, and we continued our climb toward building NSPIRE Aviation together.

Now, for the real story.

Any business needs revenue to offset its expenses, and flight schools typically do this using a plane. The only problem was we didn't have one of those and didn't have nearly the money to afford one at the time. However, we did have a solid understanding of ground school concepts and a passion for teaching, so we decided to offer ground school courses until we saved up enough cash to acquire a plane. Our first two ground school students enrolled in January 2019. One of those students was Skarleth Ayala.

Skarleth Ayala was a young mother and dental hygienist from Honduras. Skarleth had three kids, a contagious smile, and an eager mind to learn.

Skarleth dreamed of becoming a pilot like her dad. She was financially constrained yet determined to complete her training as an homage to her late father. She began her training and excelled in the course. Unfortunately, after a few months of studying, life got in the way, and she decided a college degree was a better investment for her family than a pilot's license. She left NSPIRE, but she didn't give up on her dream to fly.

Before leaving, Skarleth asked me to explore alternative ways to finance her aviation training. Unfortunately, I was out of ideas except for possibly starting a GoFundMe page where she could share her story and people could invest in her education. She was not familiar with GoFundMe, but she was willing to give it a shot.

Later that week, I received a late-night Instagram message from Skarleth. She had taken my advice and written her story down. I didn't know Skarleth's story before that day, but I could never forget it after reading it.

Skarleth's message read:

"My name is Skarleth Ayala.

I was born in Honduras, but I am now a United States citizen. I am writing this letter because it has been my dream to become a pilot.

When I was a child, my father took me to work with him to see the airplanes he was working on. He was an airplane mechanic. I loved the sounds and the smells of the planes, and I would jump at the chance to go to work with him anytime he asked. My love for planes has never subsided, it has gotten stronger. Sadly, my father passed away six years ago, and I feel the love we shared about airplanes adds to our father/daughter bond and makes my desire to become a pilot that much stronger. I want to follow my dreams of becoming a pilot as well as honoring him and his love for planes.

Please allow me to tell you more about myself.

I came to this country as an immigrant and to make a better life for myself. When I was eleven years old, my parents separated, and my mother changed. She was always upset and angry. I told myself then that I would live life to its fullest and find happiness in everything. At times, it wasn't easy to find positivity when things were so hard, but I tried. Obviously, being raised as a child in Honduras is nothing like being raised as a child from the United States. We just did not have the luxury of being a kid. We all grew up fast.

Once the school day was over, I would literally run home to do my homework and then rush off to my afternoon job. I usually worked from 4-8 each night with no dinner or food until I would get home. I had to give my pay to my family to help with bills, but I always took some out for myself and hid it from my family. I knew this was the only way I would be able to get out of my situation and be able to move to the United States. It took me four long years to save enough money and then one day, at the age of fourteen, I knew I had to make a change and do it quickly. The crime was getting so bad, and every day seemed like it was getting worse. The morning I left; my mother told me I had to get myself off to school by myself so she could take my dad to a doctor's appointment.

I made the decision to go illegally to the USA.

I grabbed my money and took a bus to Guatemala. Not many policemen were out, and the border was not too far from the bus stop. As I was walking to the border, trying to act calm, somebody grabbed me from behind and stole my backpack which had all my money. I met a leader from Honduras who took people to the USA, and I told him that I had no money because they had stolen it, and I did not want to return to my country. He understood my situation and promised to help me. He explained how he was going to make the trip.

We would take the train until we reached the border. We did not have any food or money, but I knew I had no choice but to trust him. A lot of things happened on that train. Since we had no money, we rode in an empty car where it was very cold. Others were also in that empty car, and some people did not have good intentions toward a young, scared fifteen-year-old. There were policemen who looked safe, but who also wanted to hurt and abuse me. God kept putting the right people in the way to help me- I call them angels. It was dark when the train stopped. I didn't know what to do, so I just followed the group. A bunch of us jumped off the train and started running. We were all running when someone yelled, "We have to cross the river." I just followed the group and as luck would have it, one tall, large man, told me to follow him. So, I did.

We arrived in Texas. I had never been so tired and hungry in all my life. I was cold and dirty and just exhausted. I was still very scared but found a way to hide it.

I just followed this man, and whatever he said, I did. Where he went, I was right next to him. We began to walk, and I mean walk. My feet were so tired, and the shoes I had on were torn, but I said nothing. I did not want him to leave me alone by complaining, so I kept praying. Finally, he said, "Let's rest." We found a tree to sleep under. It was uncomfortable, but at least my body and mind could just stop. We rested for about two hours, and I woke up to a scream, "RUN!"

Four immigration officers were running towards us, and we all ran in different directions. I stayed in the desert for three days by myself. I never did see that man who helped me again. I have thought about him over the years and hoped he was not caught. On the third day, I found another group and joined them only to get caught by the border patrol. I was sent back to Mexico.

Two weeks later, I found another group who was trying to leave, and this time we walked for five long days. A truck drove up one evening, and I thought it was part of the plan, but it was once again the border patrol. They grabbed all of us, and we had no chance of running.

They mistreated us, pushed us around, and put guns to our heads. I was a minor. I felt hopeless at that moment. I thought I was going to jail for a long time. Once again, luck was on my side, and prayers were answered, immigration sent me to a children's shelter.

The shelter asked if I had any family I could call, and I remembered I had a sister-in-law who lived in Atlanta. I had only known her from letters and cards she would send for holidays and birthdays. I spoke with my sister-in-law and once again, God opened another door for me. She told the shelter that she would look after me and start adoption proceedings.

God opened doors so that I could have a better life and I am grateful to all who helped me get here. I was adopted, and now I have my citizen papers. I am married and have three wonderful children. I want to give them a better life, and I want them to know that dreams do come true. I believe if you can think about it, you can achieve it.

My passion is to be a pilot not only to honor my father but because it is now my passion. Only 3%

of women worldwide become airline pilots. I would like to be one of them.

Sincerely,
Skarleth Ayala"

When I finished reading the message, I sat in silence with tears streaming down my face.

I scrolled back to the top, and as I re-read the message once more, my mind shifted to another immigrant and his treacherous journey toward the promised land.

His name is Moses.

Moses' story begins in the first chapter of Exodus. Remember Joseph from chapter one? Because of Joseph, Pharaoh granted access to the Hebrews to live in Egypt around 1700-1600 BC. Within just a few centuries, the Hebrews had multiplied greatly across Egypt. The new Pharaoh, Ramses II, considered the growing immigrant group a threat. He first subjected the Hebrews to harsh slave labor. Then, becoming increasingly paranoid of a Hebrew uprising, Pharaoh ordered his army to kill all newborn Hebrew male children. At this same time, around ~1400 BC, a Hebrew mother gave birth to a baby boy. She named him Moses. To keep her son safe from the massacre, she put her newborn baby in a reed basket and floated him down the Nile River. In an incredible turn of events, Pharaoh's daughter found the basket with the child inside and appointed Moses's biological mother to raise him on her behalf in the royal palace.

While his upbringing was Egyptian, Moses was aware of his Hebrew lineage. One day, Moses saw an Egyptian beating a Hebrew slave. Overcome by anger and in the act of passion, Moses killed the Egyptian and buried his body in the sand. When word got back to Pharaoh that Moses had killed an Egyptian citizen, Pharaoh tried to kill Moses. In fear, Moses ran for his life and spent 40 years in the desert of Midian before God revealed Himself using a burning bush, calling Moses back to Egypt to free his people.

After Moses presented God with every excuse in the book of why he wasn't the right man for the job, God recruited Moses' brother, Aaron, to assist in the mission. Finally, Moses relented and returned to Egypt.

When he arrived in Egypt, Moses caused a great commotion. Moses spoke to Pharaoh on God's behalf, warning him that plagues will come to Egypt if he did not free the Hebrews from captivity. Pharaoh's heart hardened each time Moses spoke, and ten plagues ravaged the land, including water turning to blood, frogs, lice, flies, livestock pestilence, boils, hail, locusts, and darkness. The final plague took the life of the firstborn of every household who did not heed God's instruction to put an innocent lamb's blood on the doorframe in an act we now refer to as "The Passover."

After his son died in the Passover, Pharaoh agreed to free the Hebrew slaves. Moses led them out of Egypt toward the Red Sea. Pharaoh then changed his mind and pursued Moses and the Hebrews. Not able to go around the Red Sea, Moses needed a miracle to prevent being captured by the Egyptian army. In an act of great faith and power, God told Moses to raise his staff which caused the Red Sea to part in front of them, allowing the Israelites to cross on dry land ahead of the Egyptians. After safely crossing to the other side, Moses lowered his staff, and the Red Sea swallowed Pharaoh and his army, causing them all to drown.

But Moses' story is far from over. He and the Hebrews wandered in the desert for 40 years before reaching the promised land of Canaan. I challenge you to read the rest of his account on your own. This part of Moses' story reminds me of Skarleth and her bravery to step into danger and the unknown in pursuit of reaching opportunity in a new promised land.

If you don't take the time to learn someone's story, you confine them to a narrative you've written for them. Who they are becomes nothing more than a notecard in your head. As my great friend and pastor, Jamey Dickens, says, "Narratives are dangerous because they give you permission to simplify the un-simplifiable and permit the un-permissible."

Unconsciously, I had written my narrative for Skarleth. But her actual story shattered the narrative I created for her.

Moses was much more than just a Hebrew reared in the royal household of Egypt. Moses was a mighty champion of the faith, representative of the oppressed, and deliverer of the people. Likewise, Skarleth is much more than just an international student at our flight school. Skarleth is a courageous fighter, resilient survivor, and fierce caretaker. Both Moses' and Skarleth's courage paved the way for improving their own lives and bringing about the freedom and prosperity of their people.

On this side of Heaven, I won't meet any of the Hebrew captives Moses led out of slavery in Egypt. However, I have met and hugged Skarleth's beautiful children, who enjoy a much different life than they likely would have lived in Honduras. Today, Skarleth's people are flourishing in an abundance of opportunity made possible by the grit and drive of their wonderful mother, Skarleth Ayala, a modern-day Moses.

If you would like to contribute to Skarleth's flight school tuition fund, please visit https://gofund. me/29a3e200

F.A.V.O.R. DISCUSSION QUESTIONS
CHAPTER 8

Foundation: Exodus 6:6-8 NIV "Therefore, say to the Israelites: 'I am the Lord, and I will bring you out from under the yoke of the Egyptians. I will free you from being slaves to them, and I will redeem you with an outstretched arm and with mighty acts of judgment. I will take you as my own people, and I will be your God. Then you will know that I am the Lord your God, who brought you out from under the yoke of the Egyptians. And I will bring you to the land I swore with uplifted hand to give to Abraham, to Isaac and to Jacob. I will give it to you as a possession. I am the Lord.'"

Application: Who or what holds you captive today? How can you break free?

Vision: When God calls you into a new season or place, how will you respond?

Orientation: To whom in your life is this story relevant? Write their name down and share it with them.

Name: _____

Reflection: Think back on your life. How does one of your experiences connect with Moses?

9

the art of knocking on doors

M y family loves cruises. It's one of our favorite modes of vacation. So, in the spring of 2018, I drove to meet my family in New Orleans for a cruise that left the following day. The route from Atlanta to New Orleans goes through Montgomery and Mobile, Alabama. I also noticed another town I had heard about for years but had never visited.

The small town of Tuskegee, Alabama, piqued my interest.

Just outside of Auburn sits the small town of Tuskegee, Alabama. If you've heard of Tuskegee, it is likely because of Tuskegee University, Dr. George Washington Carver, and/or the Tuskegee Airmen. While I know Tuskegee for these notable things, I know it best as the hometown of my late grandfather, Dr. Harry Winters III.

Growing up, I heard story after story of his childhood in Tuskegee. Although some contained chilling accounts of the backward ways of the South in the early 20th century, most of the stories were overwhelmingly positive and nostalgic. I felt I knew more about a place I had never visited than many places I've spent considerable time in.

That day in 2018 was my chance to see it for myself.

I planned to see my grandfather later that night in New Orleans and I was excited to tell him I had visited his hometown. However, I wanted to keep it a surprise until then, so I told only my parents my intentions to stop in Tuskegee. Dad requested if I found the house to see if they still had "sweet-smelling bushes" out front. Dad linked the scent with memories of visiting his grandmother long ago.

So, I promised I'd look for him.

Although they had no address, my parents said the house was somewhere on Elm Street. I took the Tuskegee exit on I-85 and headed toward downtown.

I knew Tuskegee consisted of a majority African American population, but I never expected to get the looks I received as I drove through town. I was an outsider, and the locals made that fact very apparent. However, it didn't faze me. I enjoy exploring places where the world says I shouldn't belong. I am a firm believer that, as humans, we are all much more alike than we are different; however, that truth does not make the glares and stares any easier to bear.

As I drove down Elm Street, I soon realized how challenging my task was. Beautiful houses lined the street on both sides. I was looking for one home on a street full of them without a picture or number to reference. The only clues I possessed were the street name and the smell of the bushes from my dad's memory. I drove down the entire street, looking at every house. Finally, I made it to the end of Elm Street and turned around to drive back by once more. As I did, one home stuck out to me more than the others.

The house called to me. Something about it seemed oddly familiar. A beautiful brick house sat near the midpoint of Elm Street. Visibly historical, she had seen better days but was well-maintained and charming, nonetheless.

I parked my car across the street and walked toward the house. I had come this far, so I might as well press my luck. Walking up the steps, I took a deep breath and knocked on the door.

My heart began to beat quicker.

A few moments after my initial knocks, I heard the door begin to unlock. A middle-aged African American woman answered the door.

"Can I help you?" she asked in a kind but stern tone.

"Um, yes, ma'am. Good morning. I'm sorry to bother you. What I am about to say might sound weird, but I think my grandfather grew up in your house."

She seemed puzzled. Was I at the wrong house? Talk about embarrassing.

"Son is your grandfather Dr. W—w—win..."

"Dr. Winters," I said. "Yes ma'am, he sure is."

"Come on in, sweetheart," she said as she opened the door for me.

I reached out my hand to introduce myself. The woman told me her name is Olivia. I walked through the foyer and was immediately greeted by another, much older woman who introduced herself as Dorothy, Olivia's mother. I noticed birthday decorations in the house, so I asked whose birthday it was. Dorothy turned 89-years-old that week. I wished her a happy early birthday before sitting down for a cup of tea.

"What brought you to Tuskegee, Hamilton?" Dorothy asked me.

"My grandfather, Dr. Harry Winters, grew up in this house. I've heard about this place my entire life, but I've never had the opportunity to stop by and see it. I'm actually on my way to see him in New Orleans."

"That's just splendid." They said, "Please tell your grandfather we said hello. We've heard he is a fine man."

"I certainly will," I said. "Can I ask you a strange question?"

"Sure. What's on your mind?" Olivia responded.

Gingerly, I asked, "Do you have pecan trees in your backyard?"

Olivia looked at her mother and smiled. "We sure do. How did you know that?"

"My grandfather told me all about them. Did you know Dr. George Washington Carver used to eat dinner with my great grandparents once a week in this house?" I asked.

"I had no idea. That's incredible," Olivia said.

"I don't have the photo with me, but a photo existed of my great grandfather, Dr. Harry Winters II, and Dr. Carver in the backyard of this house many decades ago. One of the pecan trees blew over in the light wind, so my great grandfather, Dr. Harry Winters II, called his close friend, Dr. Carver, to investigate. In the photo, a metal rod is sticking out of the ground. Dr. Carver used the rod to discover bedrock just underneath the trees had caused its root system to grow out rather than down. The tree was no match for even a mild wind."

"Incredible," she said, nearly speechless.

"One more question," I said. "Did you know a member of the band "The Commodores" bought this home from my great grandmother?"

She clapped her hands and chuckled.

"I did know that one! Honey, I was married to one of the Commodores," Olivia said. "We have a son together. When my ex-husband moved to New Zealand, he left me this house. Wow, you do know a lot about this place!"

Olivia and Dorothy walked me through the house and property. We chatted for the next hour or two while flipping through family photo albums and finishing no less than two pots of tea. I remember few afternoons as vividly or fondly as this one I spent with these two sweet souls. I took a picture with them to show to my grandfather upon arrival in New Orleans. He was elated to see that his old home was still in good condition and filled with loving people like Olivia and Dorothy.

It would have been much easier to keep driving and simply say I "saw" my grandfather's childhood home, but I would have missed an opportunity to understand

and connect with what and who sat inside. Instead, I chose to get off the beaten path, take a chance, and knock on the door of a house I'd never seen before. That decision earned me two friends, a whole lot of memories, and most importantly, put a smile on my late grandfather's face.

Now that he's gone, I'd give anything to see that grin again.

In Matthew 7, toward the end of Jesus's most famous sermon, the Sermon on the Mount, Christ challenged his followers to do three things: ask, seek, and knock.

Promises await believers on the other side of these actions. Those who ask will be given. Those who seek will find. Those who knock will have doors opened for them.

I find it to be no coincidence that these verses come right after the call for believers not to judge one another by a measure they would not want to be judged.

"Do not judge, or you too will be judged. For in the same way you judge others, you will be judged, and with the measure you use, it will be measured to you." Matt 7:1-3 NIV

As I drove into Tuskegee, I felt judged. I felt like an outsider. I felt unwanted.

The more I reflected on my grandfather's stories of his upbringing in Tuskegee, the more I realized that the African American community in Tuskegee had been treated this way in their own hometown for decades.

Ms. Dorothy was the same age as my grandfather. I'm not sure if she was reared there or not, but I can imagine that if she and my grandfather were in Tuskegee simultaneously, they would have had two vastly different experiences.

One of Paw Paw's stories I remember most vividly was how influential community members attempted to bully my great grandfather, the local physician, into joining a prevalent hate group I will not name. Dr. Winters II refused to participate at the expense of his business and his livelihood. It sickens me to think that society at the time expected even Dr. Carver, a gifted black man revered for his discoveries and inventions, to enter through the back door of my great-grandparents' house just to have dinner with his two white friends.

What a different and better world we live in now.

In beautiful contrast, I was warmly welcomed through the front door of the same home to share tea and life with two black ladies who quickly became my friends.

This is mercy; this is grace. I witnessed Dr. King's dream coming true.

Seeking means not being content with my curiosity but asking the questions that make me curious. Finding means not stopping at what I found but continuing to question why I sought to find it in the first place and what to do with it now that I've found it. Knocking means not just checking the box on an experience but living it and milking it for all it's worth. On the other side of earnest seeking, finding, and knocking is a life I have never dreamed I'd live full of promises no one else could fulfill but God Himself.

F.A.V.O.R. DISCUSSION QUESTIONS
CHAPTER 9

Foundation: Matthew 7:7-8 NIV "Ask and it will be given to you; seek and you will find; knock and the door will be opened to you. For everyone who asks receives; the one who seeks finds; and to the one who knocks, the door will be opened."

Application: How are you seeking, finding, and knocking in your relationship with God today?

Vision: What doors do you anticipate God opening in your future?

Orientation: To whom in your life is this story relevant? Write their name down and share it with them.

Name: _____

Reflection: Think back on your life. How does one of your experiences connect with Jesus's teaching?

10
the art of eating alone

One day in the fall of 2018, I decided to take myself on a lunch date. A few meetings had fallen through, so my calendar was wide open. I remembered seeing an Urban Cookhouse, a fast-casual farm-to-table restaurant, down the street from my apartment. I had eaten at one in Montgomery, Alabama, and fell in love with its veggie quesadilla. Cars filled the parking lot in front of the restaurant, so I pulled into the adjacent lot belonging to CVS pharmacy. As I turned into the pharmacy lot, I nearly ran over an older gentleman walking in my blind spot. Thankfully, I saw him at the last second and slammed on the brakes.

We both shared a classic "sorry about that" wave, and I pulled forward into one of the empty parking spots.

As I was getting out of my car, the man approached my car.

"Did you go to Ole Miss?" the man asked.

"Yessir," I replied. "How did you know?"

"Your front license plate gave it away," he said, pointing at the metal plate on my 4Runner.

I had installed a pewter, Ole Miss front license plate on my car when I attended Ole Miss for grad school in 2016.

"To be honest, I forgot I even had that on there," I said.

"I attended Auburn, but I'll never forget watching Archie Manning and the Rebs play against Tennessee when I was in college. I am 72-years-old now, so it's been a while." The Ole Miss fans all wore buttons reading "Archie Who?" on them.

Do you know about "Archie Who?" he asked.

I replied, "Yes, sir. As a child, my grandmother in Mississippi used to sing me a song called "Archie Who" about that same story."

For context, Archie Manning was a no-name player going into his tenure as the quarterback at Ole Miss in the late 1960s. Opposing fans taunted the quarterback by sarcastically chanting, "Archie, who?" That was until Archie Manning became one of the greatest quarterbacks in the history of college football. Ole Miss's fan base decided to turn the tables on their rivals' joke; thus, the "Archie Who" movement was born.

Holding out his hand toward mine, the man said, "My name is Art."

"Nice to meet you, Mr. Art. My name is Hamilton Winters," I replied. "I'm going to grab a bite to eat, but thanks for stopping to say hello."

I walked into the restaurant, put in my order for a veggie quesadilla, and sat down at the bar. As most people are, I was glued to my phone while waiting for my food to arrive. Peripherally, I noticed Mr. Art came into the restaurant, ordered, and sat down behind me at a table. Just like in Washington and Toronto, I felt that unexplainable "tap" sensation on my shoulder. But, this time, the tap came with instructions. A gut-wrenching feeling prompted me to do something I would have never done under normal circumstances.

It said to me, "Take your tray, sit with him, and ask him."

"Ask him what?" I thought.

"He has something to tell you."

Weird. Should I do it? What did I have to lose?

I scoped the situation out for a minute, assessing the situation and reading Art's body language. Then, as the waitress put my quesadilla in front of me, I turned around and said across the restaurant, "Mr. Art, are you expecting anyone today?"

"Nope, just me," he replied.

"Mind if I bring my tray to your table and eat with you?" I said.

"Of course not, come on over," he replied.

I sat down, arranged my silverware and meal before me, looked him straight in the eyes, and said, "Mr. Art, I know this probably sounds insane, but I think God told me to come to sit with you because you have something to tell me."

Whew. It was out. The ball was not in my court anymore. I have no idea where this was going, but I did it.

I obeyed. He probably thought I was mental.

Art didn't skip a beat. Grinning, he said, "Boy, do I have something to tell you."

Goosebumps covered every inch of my body.

"Hamilton, a few months ago, I went on a bike ride. Each year, I participate in a bike ride across the state of Georgia. A few of us go on a practice ride to get back into the groove of things before the official race later in the year. The practice ride took place on a beautiful, sunny morning just south of Athens, Georgia. The birds were singing and there wasn't a cloud in the sky.

Or so I've been told.

I don't remember any of it. A few minutes into the ride, I collapsed and went into full cardiac arrest. I was completely unconscious, not breathing. No one in my group had medical experience. I should have died right there.

Instead, three emergency room doctors from Piedmont Hospital in Atlanta happened to be stopped a few yards ahead of us, plagued by an unusual flat tire. Amazing, right? It gets better."

Already blown away, I thought to myself, how could it get any better?

Then Art said, "Those doctors did something miraculous to me that day. The rule of thumb is to give up if the patient does not respond within ten minutes or less of administering CPR. These doctors resuscitated me for more than twenty minutes. I might be sharing too much information, but during my resuscitation, I vomited everywhere. These doctors continued to give me mouth-to-mouth regardless."

He continued, "I'm an old man, Hamilton. Naturally, I see just about every kind of doctor there is to see. I asked each one of my doctors to review the facts of what happened that day, and if they're willing, to write a letter explaining their findings. Every single one of them said I should have died that day because any responsible medical professional would have given up on me.

Fortunately, these three doctors didn't give up, and that's why I'm able to sit here and tell you this story today.

I have no doubt God brought you over here to hear this story. You're going to get the chance to save someone's life one day. And when you do, it's imperative that no matter how much you want to, you don't stop trying. Even when you get tired, or you think there's just no hope, keep going. If those doctors hadn't defied the rule of thumb for me, I wouldn't be here today. It's funny, it's been four or five months since that ride, and each day I have made it my mission to tell as many people about it as will listen.

You're the first person who has ever asked to hear it without me prompting them to listen."

In chapter 11 of John's Gospel, a man named Lazarus fell severely ill. Jesus loved Lazarus and his two sisters, Mary and Martha, very much. The sisters sent word of their brother's illness to Jesus, who was away at the time. Rather than go to Bethany to heal Lazarus, Jesus chose to wait. His decision confused and frustrated both the disciples and the two sisters, but Jesus knew something they didn't.

Lazarus died four days before Jesus arrived in Bethany. Both Mary and Martha make a point of Jesus's tardiness, reminding Jesus that had he come right away, Lazarus would not have died. Gracefully, Jesus assures the sisters that Lazarus will rise once again.

A crowd amassed and began to wonder, "Could not he who opened the eyes of the blind man have kept this man from dying?" John 11:37

Rather than justify his actions to the crowd, Jesus instead focused on the heart of the matter: faith.

Before performing his miracle, Jesus prayed, giving thanks to God for hearing his prayers and giving him the power to prove God's authority on Earth. Then, Jesus called in a loud voice, "Lazarus, come out!"

Immediately, in front of the entire crowd, a man wrapped in linen with a cloth covering his face walked out of the tomb, alive.

More than Art and Lazarus dying and being revived to life again is the connection between seeing, believing, and telling. In both cases, death was preventable. Art could have been evaluated beforehand by one of his many doctors, put on a medication regimen or a different diet, and quickly finished the bike ride. Likewise, Jesus could have immediately made the two-mile journey to Bethany to heal his friend Lazarus instantly after hearing of his illness.

However, preventing death doesn't make as strong a testimony. The impact of their witness exponentially increased by going from healing the sick to raising the dead.

After four days in the tomb, Mary and Martha should have expected Jesus to give the eulogy for Lazarus instead of raising him from the dead. After more than ten minutes of CPR and mouth-to-mouth, the doctors should have given up as many would have a long time before. Yet, in both cases, the sisters and the doctors believed that a miracle could happen. It was faith that laid a foundation for the miraculous to occur.

I can only speculate, but I imagine most of the crowd went from seers to believers at that moment in Bethany. Its appearance in John's Gospel proves the story was shared with others and has now impacted billions of lives since. I also know the crowd surrounding Art that day on the road's shoulder went from seers to believers when Art began to breathe again. The number of lives Art's story has impacted since he, his family, and those directly involved in his miracle have shared it is innumerable. While I will never know the total number, I know it's at least one.

That person is me.

After reading this book, that number will rise to two, and your passing along this story will increase the number even further. It's challenging to keep an account of miraculous healing to yourself. It's even harder not to share a story of the dead coming back to life. Jesus knew this.

As the world looked on, thinking Jesus left chips on the table by letting Lazarus die, Jesus knew he was crafting a much bigger testimony for Lazarus to share. I can imagine Art's case was the same.

Sometimes the best way to bring life to others is through death. No one knows this better than Jesus Himself, who willingly died so he could provide eternal life to all who accept it.

Just think, I could have eaten lunch anywhere and with anyone in the world that day. But, instead, I chose to eat alone, or I thought I did.

But God had a bigger story to tell.

F.A.V.O.R. DISCUSSION QUESTIONS
CHAPTER 10

Foundation: John 11:41-44 "...Then Jesus looked up and said, 'Father, I thank you that you have heard me. I knew that you always hear me, but I said this for the benefit of the people standing here, that they may believe that you sent me.' When he had said this, Jesus called in a loud voice, 'Lazarus, come out!' The dead man came out, his hands and feet wrapped with strips of linen, and a cloth around his face."

Application: Has Jesus raised you to new life in him? If so, how are you living your new life differently today than you used to live? If not, what is holding you back?

Vision: How will you use your story to bring life to those still in the grave?

Orientation: To whom in your life is this story relevant? Write their name down and share it with them.

Name: _____

Reflection: Think back on your life. How does one of your experiences connect with Lazarus?

11
the art of ride sharing

My sister, Hollin, is one of my best friends in the world, and we've only grown closer with age. Hollin studied abroad during the summer of 2019 before her last year of college. Having studied abroad myself during the summer of 2016, Hollin asked my advice on where she should go. She was choosing between Rome or Cape Town, South Africa.

I lobbied for Cape Town, and thankfully, she took my advice.

Hollin spent four great weeks in South Africa with a group of strangers who quickly became some of her closest friends. Hollin is an early July baby, and her 21st birthday happened to fall on the last week of her study abroad experience. When my parents asked what she wanted for her birthday, she said she wanted me to come to South Africa and spend it with her.

I willingly obliged.

Hollin and I spent a fantastic week in Cape Town together. She must have told her friends much about me beforehand because they took me in as if I had been on their trip with them the entire time. The group consisted of 80 American college students, and more than 70 of them were girls. I served as the "big brother" of the group.

Throughout my time in Cape Town, Hollin showed me all that the city had to offer. From the Old Biscuit Mill to Hout Bay, we soaked it all in. I could tell countless stories about our time in and around Cape Town, but this story is about my attempt to leave.

Everyone in Hollin's program, myself included, flew out within an hour of one another. On Sunday night, July 7, 72 of the students, including Hollin, boarded the KLM flight to Amsterdam departing at 11:00 PM. The other eight students and staff were on my Air France flight to Paris, departing at 11:45 PM.

I knew the students would want to say their goodbyes before loading up the tour buses to depart from the airport. They invited me to ride the bus with them, but two thoughts crossed my mind:

Selflessly, I don't want my presence to take away from the goodbye of friends who will likely never see each other again.

Selfishly, I can beat them to the airport and through security instead of waiting in line with eighty other people.

With this in mind, I decided to order an Uber.

The Uber driver picked me up around 9:00 PM from our hotel, and we departed for the airport. The drive was supposed to take around 25 minutes. Unfortunately, my driver spoke little English, so we spent most of the time in silence.

We were nearing the airport when I began to hear a sputtering sound coming from the car. The sound started faint, but it grew louder as we continued forward. Finally, the vehicle started shaking violently, and we quickly pulled to the side of the highway.

The driver turned around to me with worry in his eyes. Then, frantically he motioned toward the front of the car, saying, "Water. Engine. Water."

I was beyond confused at this point and frustrated at the inconvenience.

"Gas?" I asked. "Do you mean you ran out of gas?"

I'm thinking to myself, "If this guy picked me up on an empty tank, and now we're stranded on the side of a South African highway, Uber isn't going to hear the end of this."

July marks the middle of winter in the southern hemisphere, so it was pitch black in South Africa by this time at night.

The only lights I could see came from a few scattered streetlights and the headlights of cars driving past us. Not only did the driver not get out of the car, but he turned the car's lights off as soon as we parked!

He had barely pulled off the roadway. I could feel our car shake as vehicles whizzed past us. I had seen too many videos of cars being rear-ended on dark interstates by unsuspecting motorists to let this guy get us killed.

"Put your flashers on, please! We're going to get killed," I pleaded desperately.

He refused.

I continued to stare out of the back windshield of the Toyota Camry, watching and waiting for the car that would signal the end for us. I simultaneously ordered a second Uber to pick me up from the first one.

I unlocked my door and asked the driver to open the trunk to get my luggage out. The driver immediately re-locked all the doors and said, "No. No. Stay in the car."

By this point, I'm pretty mad. Not only is this a significant inconvenience, but the driver is also holding me against my will.

"Why?" I asked with a stern tone of voice.

"No. Please, no," he said.

Begrudgingly, I listened.

Side note: Did you know that the Uber app won't let you drop a pin just anywhere? I didn't know until I needed to drop one on the side of a random South African highway.

Anyways, back to the story.

Since the road's shoulder was unregistered on the Uber app, the pin I dropped was redirected to another location, causing my second driver to get lost trying to find me. I watched the car icon on the map go in circles until I got a phone call from the driver asking me what side of the Salvation Army building I was on.

"Salvation Army?" I asked, "No, I'm on the side of the interstate! I'm inside another Uber right now. We broke down on the side of the highway. I'd tell you what I see, but I don't see anything. Just darkness."

"Okay," he said, "Don't move. I'm coming to get you." Just then, two tour buses passed us.

"Well, there goes Hollin and friends," I thought to myself. "They'll not only beat me to the airport and through security, but they also got a free ride while I'll have to pay for two of them!"

Ten minutes later, a car pulled onto the shoulder behind us. The driver called me to tell me he was sitting behind us. I told the first driver that my other ride had arrived, and I needed to retrieve my belongings now.

Before letting me out, the first driver looked me straight in the eyes and said one word, "Hurry."

He unlocked the doors and popped the trunk. I grabbed my bags and got in the other car as quickly as I could. The first driver ran over to the second driver, pleading with him for water. Having a spare bottle in his console, the second driver handed the water to the first driver, and we sped off to the airport.

"Sir, can you tell me what happened?" the new driver asked me, puzzled.

I told him the story.

"Wow. Not good. Not good at all, sir," he said. I could tell the story bothered him, but I didn't know why. I didn't inquire.

We spent the rest of the ride in intense silence. Then, finally, I got out, tipped the driver in cash, and caught up with Hollin in the security line.

"We saw you on the side of the road," Hollin said. "Are you okay?"

A bit shaken up and still frustrated, I told her what happened. She was shocked.

We all went through the security checkpoint and met back up on the other side. An hour or so passed, and the KLM flight began to board. I hugged all my new friends and Hollin goodbye. Then, I watched as their big, blue 747 taxied out for the runway.

At that same time, our Air France flight began to board. A few groups were already on the jet bridge when I heard the strange announcement come over the intercom.

"Attention passengers on Air France Flight 871 service to Paris, this flight has been canceled due to a malfunction with the aircraft. Please return to baggage claim for more details."

I stopped dead in my tracks. Did I hear that correctly?

Everyone else at the gate seemed to go about their business as usual. A group of Hollin's study abroad students and staff were standing a few yards away from me. I walked over to them and asked, "Did you guys just hear that announcement?"

"What announcement? We didn't hear anything," the group responded.

Oh no. This isn't good, I thought to myself.

"I hate to be the bearer of bad news, but they just canceled our flight," I said.

A blank stare covered their faces as they looked at me in disbelief.

"You're kidding me, right?" the group director asked with a tone reminding me of the cab driver in Washington, D.C. when I misplaced my wallet.

In both cases, I wished I was.

For the passengers who heard the initial announcement, reality had not yet set in. Remember, it was midnight on a Sunday night. Everyone just wants to get to their seat, go to sleep, and start their day-long journey home.

The gate agent came back on the intercom for a second announcement. "Attention passengers of Air France Flight 871 service to Paris, again, this flight has been canceled. Please return to baggage claim. If you live in Cape Town, please go home. If you do not have a place to stay, please see the booking agent in baggage claim for hotel accommodations."

We could see the KLM flight taking off through the window of our gate. They would have no idea what happened to us until they reached Amsterdam. Boy, I wish I had a seat on that bird. Instead, I am stranded in Cape Town.

We walked down to baggage claim and waited another hour or so in line for hotel accommodations. Then, all of a sudden, each of us received a text message from Air France. It was our new respective itinerary. The news explained that the next Air France flight out of Cape Town wasn't until the following Friday, so we had been automatically rerouted home sometime over the next couple of days.

No two people in the group had the same route home—one student connected through Rome, one through Abu Dhabi, one through Addis Ababa, Ethiopia. My route sent me to Johannesburg, South Africa, at 9:00 AM the next day. The only problem was it was already the next day.

We took a bus back to Cape Town proper and stood in line for another hour with all the other Air France passengers before getting our hotel room keys. By the time I got to my hotel room, I only had two and a half hours to sleep before I needed to wake up and call a third Uber to the airport within twelve hours.

On my morning ride to the airport, I scanned the shoulder of the road, trying to recognize where I broke down the night before. Everything looked much different during the daytime than it did at night. Finally, I spotted the location where we had pulled over.

I drew the spot to my driver's attention and told him what had happened. He looked at me in the rearview mirror in absolute horror.

"Sir, are you sure you broke down here?" he asked.

"Yes. I'm positive," I said, continuing, "My driver turned off his lights and refused to turn on his flashers. I just knew we were going to get rear-ended. We were sitting ducks."

"Sir, I don't think you understand," he said, trying to be as respectful as possible.

"Sir, look around," he said.

I turned my head from right to left. Shacks and tin roofs lined both sides of the interstate for as far as I could see.

"I just see a bunch of metal sheds and shacks," I said.

"Precisely, sir. This area of Cape Town is called Nyanga. Nyanga is one of the most dangerous townships in the entire country. As drivers, we know to never stop here. This township is notorious for seizing stopped cars by force. However, by turning off the lights and keeping you in the car, that driver likely saved your life last night.

God is watching out for you, sir."

Between the 9th and 8th centuries BC, the prophet Jonah lived in the Northern Kingdom of Israel. God called upon Jonah to travel to the wicked capital of Assyria, Nineveh, to warn its inhabitants of God's impending wrath if they did not repent. Jonah, despising the Ninevites and rejecting God's command, fled God's mission by boarding a ship to Tarshish. On the journey, the ship encountered a terrible storm leading the crew to question if God was angry with one of the members on board. The sailors cast lots pointing to Jonah as the culprit. Jonah admitted that it was he who had disobeyed God and brought upon this terrible storm. He asked the crew to throw him overboard.

As Jonah sank to the bottom of the sea, a large fish swallowed him. Inside the fish, Jonah prayed and begrudgingly agreed to obey God by going to Nineveh, and the fish spit him out on the shore. Jonah then visited Nineveh, preached against it, and succeeded in getting the city to repent of its sin; however, Jonah's disdain for Nineveh remained.

Rather than staying and celebrating the fact that the people of Nineveh had turned from their sin, Jonah decided to flee the city and wait outside its walls, hopeful that God's destruction would still reign down on the town God sent him to save. To Jonah's dissatisfaction, God spared Nineveh and used this time as a teaching moment for the prophet. First, God caused a plant to miraculously grow beside Jonah to provide him shade from the sun to prove a point. Then, God sent a worm to eat the plant, causing it to wither and die. Then God sent a scorching wind and a blistering amount of sun. Jonah wanted to die and complained to the Lord.

But the Lord responded, "You have been concerned about this plant, though you did not tend it or make it grow. It sprang up overnight and died overnight. And should I not have concern for the great city of Nineveh, in which there are more than a hundred and twenty thousand people who cannot tell their right hand from their left—and also many animals?" Jonah 4:10-11 NIV

While we don't get a conclusion to the story, we can only surmise that Jonah realized at this moment that he was put on trial and found guilty of not offering the same mercy and grace that Jonah himself required.

Inconvenienced by God's commission, Jonah fled. Jonah's running caused him to become stranded at sea. Jonah's abandonment at sea wouldn't save Nineveh, so God sent a fish to swallow him and deliver him to the shore. Jonah's decision to reluctantly obey God inside the fish ultimately saved Nineveh but displeased Jonah. Jonah's displeasure and discomfort opened the door for a teaching moment from God and ultimately saved Jonah from himself.

Yes, God saved Nineveh using Jonah, but ironically, God saved Jonah using Nineveh.

Thankfully, this is not a story of my fleeing from God's will, and thankfully, I've never been on a battered ship at sea, swallowed by a fish, or spit out onshore. However, I did find myself in a foreign land, inconvenienced on my trip, and unwilling to display the same mercy to my driver as I required from God.

Only after Jonah's lesson with the plant could he realize the God who inconvenienced him by sending him to Nineveh saved him from himself. Likewise, only after my third rideshare to the airport in 12 hours did I realize, the person I thought was inconveniencing me, my driver had saved me from the dangers I didn't know surrounded me at the time.

More than anything else, he saved me from me.

How clear it seems to look back on the situation, but at the moment, it's often difficult to recognize the lesson God is trying to teach us. If we are grace recipients, we must also be grace givers.

Jonah and I both required and received God's grace, yet we were both unwilling at the time to extend the same grace to the individuals who God had placed in our path to save us.

Curious, I looked back in the app to see what my driver's name was since I partially owe my life to him.

His name is "Beloved."

I couldn't make this stuff up if I tried.

F.A.V.O.R. DISCUSSION QUESTIONS
CHAPTER 11

Foundation: Jonah 4:1, 4 "But to Jonah this seemed very wrong, and he became angry... But the Lord replied, 'Is it right for you to be angry?'"

Application: Are you following God's will for your life today or fleeing from it?

Vision: How will you give grace in inconvenient situations to come?

Orientation: To whom in your life is this story relevant? Write their name down and share it with them.

Name: _____

Reflection: Think back on your life. How does one of your experiences connect with Jonah?

12
the art of getting stuck

If you're reading this, you made it through the year 2020. Among pandemics, hurricanes, wildfires, and political unrest, the year proved bizarre. Of all the negatives 2020 brought with it, some positives emerged. One positive was that remote work became not only widely accepted but encouraged and even required during the pandemic. In spring 2020, the lockdown started in the United States. My then-girlfriend, Alix, and I planned a trip to Puerto Rico, hoping the restrictions would lift by our departure date in August. Unfortunately, as time drew near, the outlook of our journey became increasingly dire.

We decided to cancel.

Alix and I love to travel internationally; however, our inability to leave the country during 2020 gave us a new motivation to see parts of the United States we had not seen before.

In mid-July, I woke up in the middle of the night with the idea to plan an epic road trip. I had recently turned down my dream promotion at the marketing firm I worked at to pursue a calling into ministry leadership and seminary. I didn't know much about what I was stepping into, but I knew on September 4th, 2020, I'd be released of all my work responsibilities, and I already had a flight to Los Angeles booked to see my sister, Hollin, for Labor Day. If I could convince Alix to entertain the road trip, and if she could convince her company to let her work remotely for a few weeks, we might just pull it off.

I spent the next three hours of the night researching every Western U.S. road trip itinerary I could find. I put a rough plan together and counted down the minutes until I could call Alix and pitch it to her. When I finally called her, Alix sounded hesitant. She knows me better than anyone and knows I tend to get excited about plans quickly. I saw through her initial hesitancy and pressed on. Regardless of her reaction, I knew I had piqued her interest.

Over the next few days, I diligently worked to piece together a realistic plan and budget for our trip. We would spend twenty-two days in a converted campervan. I found a company that allowed us to pick the van up in Los Angeles and drop it off in Las Vegas by paying a small one-way fee. We'd start our journey in L.A. and drive up the Pacific Coast Highway to Big Sur before cutting over to Yosemite. Next, we'd drive through San Francisco to Redwoods National Park then over to Crater Lake in Oregon from Yosemite. From Oregon, we'd cut across Idaho to Yellowstone and down through The Grand Tetons and Jackson Hole, Wyoming. Then, we'd cut through Salt Lake City, Utah to Moab, Utah for Arches and Canyonlands National Parks before hitting the Grand Canyon on our way through Bryce Canyon toward Zion National Park. After Zion, we'd make the trek back to Nevada using whatever time we had left, enjoying the sights and sounds of the Las Vegas Strip.

Sounds magical, right?

I thought so. I sold it. HARD. Alix bought it, and so did her company. After getting the corporate green light, we put a deposit down for the campervan and booked our flights.

A few weeks before we departed for California, 2020 struck again. California and Oregon were set ablaze with wildfires. I checked the weather every hour of every day until I lost service after takeoff, praying for good news. When we landed in Los Angeles, smoke filled the sky. We spent a few days with Hollin in Los Angeles before embarking on our road trip. Each day, the sky looked smokier than the day before.

It didn't look good.

On Saturday, we picked up the campervan. Three other campervans had just returned to the depot after being denied entry through San Francisco due to wildfires. We were supposed to visit San Francisco on Monday. Unfortunately, Snapchat and Instagram posts from the Bay Area showed an ominous orange sky on an otherwise clear day. It looked like hell. That same day, a new fire sparked near Big Sur, where we'd planned to travel through the very next day.

Was our trip ruined?

We needed to make an executive decision. Do we risk it all and keep with our original plan? Or do we call an audible? After looking at the wildfire maps and weather for the upcoming week, we decided to flip our route on its head and drive it the opposite way. The new course would not only get us out of the immediate wildfire danger, but it would also buy us a couple of weeks for fires to die down near our originally planned stops to hit on the back end of our trip.

Instead of going northwest through California, we drove northeast through Las Vegas to Zion National Park. We left early enough in the morning to camp outside the Zion gates that same night.

Zion National Park showed off. It was arguably our favorite stop on the entire trip. We didn't spend as much time there as we would have liked, but we spent long enough to whet our appetite. We camped Monday night just outside of Bryce Canyon. The sky was dazzling. You could see an entire band of the Milky Way just by looking up. I would have stayed outside all night had the temperatures not dropped so severely after sunset. Tuesday morning, we hit Bryce Canyon National Park and did our best to make it to the Utah/Arizona border before sunset.

Bryce proved much better than I initially expected. I walked away, thoroughly impressed. Bryce Canyon's famous hoodoos made the park feel extraterrestrial. Multiple lookouts on the scenic route offered otherworldly views. Alix and I completed a quick hike on Queens Garden Trail before departing the park. We had a long drive ahead of us to get to Page, but we were looking forward to it. Not only would Page offer us incredible sights in Horseshoe Bend and Lake Powell, but it would provide us with even better smells since we planned to shower there as we had not bathed since we departed Los Angeles.

Each night, Alix and I did our best to find a free campsite using various websites and blogs for guidance. The federal government owns a great deal of land in the western US and offers much of it for public use. However, most campsites have no bathroom or shower facilities. They are merely a legal parking spot for campers to stay for a few nights.

We had difficulty finding a good campsite near Page, but one spot kept popping up on nearly every site we visited. Lone Rock Beach National Recreation Area received high praise as a good option for folks traveling through the area. A $13 entry fee granted us access to plenty of campsites and unlimited use of shower and bathroom facilities. Thirteen dollars for a long-overdue shower, clean bathroom, and a place to camp? Sign me up!

In our research, we noticed a few bloggers mentioned how sandy the ground was there. The name "Lone Rock Beach" is indicative of the lakebed exposed as Lake Powell recedes throughout the year. Then, as the lake fills with water from melted snow upstream, the beach disappears again. In September, the lake nears its lowest point, so we kept in mind to stay on the road as best we could once we arrived.

We arrived at Lone Rock Beach about an hour before sunset. Alix and I had grown used to eating in the dark over the past few days, so we were excited about the possibility of showering and eating dinner while the sun was still up. We paid our admission fee to the park ranger and drove down the dirt road toward the shower facilities. The area was gorgeous. A massive boulder sits directly in the middle of the lake, and the view is breathtaking. We made the responsible decision not to attempt the drive down to the lakeshore but rather to stay near the road since our rental van wasn't equipped with 4WD.

I asked Alix if she'd prefer to shower or find a campsite first. She chose the campsite. We had passed a few good ones on our way to the facilities, so I decided to backtrack toward those. Instead of pulling into a parking space at the facility to reverse and go back the way we came, I noticed a path that circled back to the main road behind the facility.

A foot-deep washout sat just before the path met back up with the main dirt road. With as much stuff as we had stored in the van, driving over the washout would inevitably toss everything we owned onto the floor. Tire tracks were visible off to the left side of the path where others had gone around the divot. I guess they had the same thought I did. Going around the washout seemed like our best option, so I took it. The only problem was the road wasn't made of dirt.

Instead, it was sand.

We quickly found ourselves stuck up to our axles at a dangerous angle. I jumped out of the van to assess the situation. What had I done?! Alix was in disbelief.

The sun would set within the hour, and the night was forecasted to be cold. We needed to move fast. About ten minutes into our dilemma, a couple from California pulled over in their maroon Chevrolet Suburban to ask us if we needed help. Since their Suburban wasn't 4WD, it was of little assistance to us. Their willingness to help at least comforted us in this time of stress. They recommended we find the tire that spins, dig it out and place large rocks underneath it to gain traction. They then left to see if the park ranger might be able to pull us out.

A few minutes later, another truck stopped to help. They introduced themselves as Jeralyn and Bryan from Salt Lake City and attempted to pull us out using a tie rated to a thousand pounds. Being that our van weighed around 7,000 lbs., it's not surprising that the tie snapped immediately. They then offered to drive into town to purchase chains at Walmart. Interested in exploring every possible option, I gave them a hundred-dollar bill and sent them on their way.

Alix called her dad, Tim, to ask about their AAA membership. While Alix talked on the phone, a man in a silver Prius pulled up and told me a man just down the road with a maroon Dodge truck towed him the day before for $40. He recommended I walk down to the man's trailer to see what he could do for us. I immediately began my 200-yard trek down the beach. When I arrived at the trailer, I caught an older man relieving himself in some sagebrush. After finishing up and zipping his pants, the man introduced himself as Tom, a retired veteran. He told me he was diagnosed with PTSD and began to unpack a laundry list of complaints about the Department of Veterans Affairs. Time was of the essence, so I interrupted his story to explain my predicament and ask for his help. Tom called his 11-year-old mutt, Rambo, and we all got in his truck and drove to the stranded van.

By the time we returned to the van, Alix had been on the phone with AAA for quite some time. Tom got out of his truck and assessed the situation. Tom then began ranting about how dire our situation was before hooking chains up to the front of the van. Tom's negativity was making Alix grow increasingly anxious, yet he continued. "Son, I've pulled a lot of people out of this place, but I ain't never seen one as bad as this one here. You got about a 75% chance of flipping this thing, and I ain't financially responsible if it does." Alix had heard enough.

She stepped in and insisted we get a professional tow service instead of Tom from Vietnam. At this point, I agreed. I thanked Tom for his time and gave him a $20 bill for his trouble.

Tom unhooked the chains but didn't take the cue to leave. He hung around for another half hour, drawing our attention to everything we had done wrong to get ourselves stuck in the first place. I tried to ignore Tom and focus instead on the solution at hand.

Just then, I got a phone call from Jeralyn and Bryan at Walmart asking if they should purchase the chains they found. After concurring with Alix—still on the phone with AAA—I told them we decided to go with a professional tow service instead. Still, I appreciated their willingness to help us.

When it seemed like things couldn't get much worse, the AAA representative told Alix they couldn't help us, and we would have to pay for the tow service out of pocket. Alix then called the rental van company. Their "helpline" was anything but helpful.

With what little internet service I had, I used my phone to google towing companies nearby. The only tow company in the area was in Kanab, Utah. Kanab was more than an hour away from us, but there was no other option.

I called and spoke with a man named Jake. After describing our situation, Jake said we would need their specialty truck which was currently out on an emergency call and wouldn't be available until the following day at the earliest. At $175/hour for what was likely going to be a three-hour ordeal, getting stuck was turning out to be an expensive little mistake.

To exhaust every option, I called my insurance agent to see if they had alternative options. I was transferred to an automated message and then sent to a third-party roadside assistance person who, after talking with her for 15 mins, told me I needed to speak with an agent. I'd come full circle and have nothing but wasted time to show for it. The sun had set, and the elements had begun to set in. The temperature was dropping quickly.

After AAA had turned her down, Alix called the same tow truck company as I had to see if she could get someone to come before tomorrow morning. I prayed for a miracle while waiting on hold for what seemed like an eternity. Then I was transferred to an after-hours agent who spoke very little English and could barely hear what I was saying due to my waning cell service. After painfully extracting my information, he assured me someone would be on the way immediately. I got an automated text message saying a tow truck would arrive at 9:05 PM.

Looking down the main road, I saw headlights driving toward us. Jeralyn and Bryan pulled up next to us, rolled their windows down, and returned the cash. I thanked them for their time and for trying to help us. Not wanting to ruin their trip, I told them not to worry about us; we would be fine. But they refused to leave.

I conferred with Alix, who was beyond stressed out by the entire ordeal. All she wanted to do was stay with the van and our belongings until we found a solution. Acting as the middleman, I told Jeralyn and Bryan that Alix didn't want to leave and tried to send them on their way not to ruin their vacation any more than we already had. Instead, they offered to take us into town to stay at a hotel for the night. Once more, they refused to abandon us. Instead, they offered to stay with us as long as it took to find a solution.

I gladly accepted their company.

At that point, I was interrupted by a call from the towing company. Could this be good news? I answered and recognized Jake's voice from earlier. "Hi, we're calling about your Jeep Grand Cherokee that's stuck. Where are you?" Jake said.

Ahh, come on. The insurance company's after-hours representative must have told them my Jeep (the primary car on the insurance policy) was stuck. However, I told him, and he repeated back to me that we were driving a campervan.

I tried to re-explain the situation to Jake, but after recognizing who I was, Jake turned irate. He proceeded to chew me out for a good 10 minutes about how he's been called four times about this same campervan, and he's tired of us annoying him.

"For the last time, man, tomorrow morning is the best we can do! Quit calling me!" he said and hung up.

We had exhausted all our options at this point. It's dark, it's cold, and we're still stuck.

Thankfully, Alix didn't stop trying. She called AAA one more time, seeking clarity as to why they would not cover our situation under her policy. Alix put the call on speakerphone so we could hear what happened.

"So, it's a campervan, not an RV?" asked the lady on the other end of the call.

"Correct. It's a standard van, just converted to camp in," Alix replied.

"Oh, in that case, it does qualify for coverage. The last person you spoke with must have cataloged your van as an RV. Sorry about that," the representative responded.

Behold! The break we needed. Now, all we needed to do is figure out where we'd sleep for the night and pray hard that the tow truck could get us unstuck in the morning.

Jeralyn and Bryan motioned me over to their truck.

"Hey man, we were just talking," said Bryan, "and if you guys have cushions in the van, you should just lay them down in the back of our truck and camp with us for the night. We have food, extra blankets, warm coats, and cold beer."

At this point, I recognized Jeralyn and Bryan were angels sent to save us. My prayer had been (partially) answered. While our van was still stuck, God had provided a place for us to stay for the night. The door was opening for an incredible night with two new amazing friends. Another invitation that we needed to say "Yes" to experience. The hard part would be convincing Alix to trust me and go along with the plan.

Understandably, Alix had had enough.

She was tired, frustrated, and anxious. Not to mention, she was expected to be awake and logged onto her computer working by 5:00 AM the following morning.

Alix was willing to sacrifice almost anything to maintain whatever consistency she could get her hands on. The van and her belongings represented consistency, so she initially insisted that we camp next to our van.

In my mind, the choice was obvious. To me, it was foolish to choose to sleep out in the cold next to a van full of stuff we can't even use rather than accept a miraculous invitation from strangers to camp with them for the night.

But I couldn't judge Alix. She had done more than I could have ever asked of her.

I just needed her to trust me one more time.

Throughout the entire ordeal, I maintained an overwhelming sense of peace. It felt very similar to my experiences in Washington, Toronto, Hong Kong,

Bali, Malaysia, and South Africa. God worked things out for me all over the globe, and I had faith that God was working things out in Page, UT, too.

But, just like most things in life, there was no guarantee.

What I could offer was a smile on my face and positive reinforcement that everything would work out. We just had to wait and see if it would. I took Alix aside and reflected on what I said to her the night we first started dating.

"Alix, remember when I asked you to be my girlfriend? I told you the adventure would be incredible. You'd see things you never thought you'd see, do things you never thought you'd do, and feel things you never thought you'd feel. I also warned you that I'd push you outside your comfort zone, and it would be painful at times. I've told you stories about things that have happened to me throughout my life to make you smile and laugh, but they're only worth smiling and laughing about because you know everything worked out in the end.

When you're living the story, you're scared, unsure, and nervous. You're living one of those stories right now. One day, we'll tell our kids about when we got stuck in the middle of nowhere, and two strangers— angels—stopped to rescue us. I can't promise you much, but I can promise you this; I will be right next to you the entire time, and I won't let anything bad happen to you. God is working on this; I know it. I just need you to trust me.

Do you trust me?"

Graciously and nervously, Alix said yes. We unloaded the belongings we needed from the van, locked it, and hopped in the bed of Jeralyn's Toyota Tacoma. She drove us to the restroom facilities, but adrenaline was still pumping, so neither one of us felt interested in a shower or food anymore. We unloaded the belongings we needed from the van, locked it, and hopped in the bed of Jeralyn's Toyota Tacoma.

I walked into the dark bathroom, knelt in a puddle of (hopefully) water, and began to plead with God to come through as I know he can only do. Alix trusted me for the night, but she still doubted we would be pulled out safely in the morning. Instantly, an overwhelming sense of peace came over me. A kind of peace you can only find in a grimy Utah bathroom when you're out of options. God was taking care of tomorrow. All we needed to do was enjoy our time with the angels God provided for us tonight.

Jeralyn and Bryan drove us to the lakeshore, and we set up camp. Because of her early morning quickly approaching, Alix retired for the night. I stayed up, relishing the opportunity for new friendships. Jeralyn and Bryan shared their food and beer with me. We traded stories by the campfire under the stars discussing our respective upbringings, worldviews, and, most importantly, faiths.

I pulled out my phone and opened the SkyGuide app. We pointed out stars for hours, seeing who could find the farthest visible star from us. As the campfire faded and the beer ran dry, we decided to go to sleep. I had difficulty sleeping that night, not due to the trauma of the day or the stress of tomorrow, but because of how beautiful the view was of the Milky Way right above us. I've never seen so many stars in my life.

Then I remembered. Before our trip started, I told Alix I dreamed of camping under the stars. She laughed at me and said I was crazy.

Well, it looks like I got my wish.

Throughout the night, I woke up various times just to make sure the stars were still there. Looking up at that sky made all my troubles disappear, and my fears seem small. In exchange for a day that felt as if it would never end, I was rewarded with a night I wish didn't have to. The stars began to fade as the sun returned. A beautiful sunrise, indeed. For as little as I slept that night, I felt surprisingly rested. Maybe I was still working off the adrenaline? Either way, Alix and I had a big day ahead, and I gladly welcomed what energy I could muster.

Alix was 95% covered under the blanket, with only her fingers exposed to keep the computer from going inactive. Unfortunately, her computer was left running throughout the night and was nearly dead when she started working. With barely enough hotspot service to stay online, it would take a miracle for the battery to last long enough for us to get the van up and running again.

But what's one more miracle at Lone Rock Beach?

Jeralyn and Bryan brewed us coffee. We took the morning slow, but as 8:30 AM approached, we packed up our camp, and they drove us up to the van. The tow truck was more than a half-hour late but seeing that big yellow beauty drive up the dirt road was one of the sweetest sights these eyes have ever beheld. An older man, Nick, rolled down the window with a big grin on his face. "I heard you folks were stuck. Let's get you out of this mess."

Nick made it look easy. He hooked up the back of the van to his truck and slowly but methodically got us level again. I got in and followed his instructions to accelerate as he told me to. In no time, we were back on solid ground.

I asked how much I owed, and Nick said, "Not a thing. AAA covered it."

Thank God Alix made that second phone call. I gave

Nick a tip, a big hug, and took a selfie with him. I also got Nick to take a picture of Jeralyn, Bryan, Alix, and me in front of the van. A tight-knit group that less than 24 hours ago didn't know the other half existed. Now, none of us would ever forget the night we spent together under the stars at Lone Rock Beach.

Arguably the most important character in the Bible, behind Jesus, was Abraham. Abraham lived around ~2000 BC in what we believe to be present-day Iraq. Abraham, or Abram as he's referred to at the time, is introduced in Genesis chapter 11. In chapter 12, God made an extraordinary promise to Abram.

"The Lord said to Abram, 'Go from your country, your people and your father's household to the land I will show you. I will make you into a great nation, and I will bless you; I will make your name great, and you will be a blessing. I will bless those who bless you, and whoever curses you I will curse; and all peoples on earth will be blessed through you.'" Genesis 12:1-3 NIV

The 75-year-old Abram, his wife, Sarai (Sarah), and his nephew, Lot, proved faithful to the Lord and went out as God had instructed them.

While it pains me to do so, I must skip over a great deal of the storyline for the sake of time and paper; however, please go back to Genesis 12 and read what

I was unable to include up to chapter 16, as it will give you much more context for the story.

More than two decades later, in Genesis 16, we find Sarai as an old and barren woman. Not to prevent Abraham from receiving God's blessing, Sarai offered Abram her Egyptian slave girl, Hagar, to build a family through her instead.

Abram agreed, and Hagar bore him a son named Ishmael.

In chapter 17, God reinforced his chapter 12 promise by changing Abram and Sarai's names to Abraham and Sarah. God told Abraham that while his firstborn son, Ishmael, would indeed be blessed and become a great people, Ishmael was not the heir of Abraham's promise. Instead, at the age of ninety, old and barren Sarah would miraculously bear a son to her now century-old husband, Abraham.

**Fun fact: Ishmael is the Patriarch of Islam

They didn't believe it. Genesis 17:17 shows us Abraham's reaction to the news.

"Abraham fell facedown; he laughed and said to himself, 'Will a son be born to a man a hundred years old? Will Sarah bear a child at the age of ninety?' " Genesis 17:17 NIV

But it wasn't just Abraham who had difficulty believing the situation at hand. In chapter 18, three visitors mysteriously visited Abraham's tent bringing further validation of God's claim. Sarah overheard the visitors and had a similar reaction to her husband.

"Sarah laughed to herself as she thought, 'After I am worn out and my lord is old, will I now have this pleasure?' " Genesis 18:12 NIV

She would. And the child's name was Isaac. It was through Isaac that God established his covenant with Abraham and fulfilled the chapter 12 promise.

Again, I hate to do this, but for the sake of the story, I must fast forward to chapter 22. So please go back and fill in for context.

By chapter 22, at Sarah's request, Abraham had sent Hagar and Ishmael out from his household, and Isaac had grown into a young man. Just as it seemed as though the story was beginning to make sense; God threw a curveball. He tested Abraham's faith.

"Take your son, your only son, whom you love— Isaac— and go to the region of Moriah. Sacrifice him there as a burnt offering on a mountain I will show you." Genesis 22:2 NIV

How can this be? After all that Abraham and Sarah had gone through to get Isaac, now God was taking him back? If Isaac died, how would God's promise to Abraham be fulfilled? Was God going back on his word?

Just as he had in earlier chapters, Abraham trusted God and went where God sent him. Although God had come through in the past, Abraham had no guarantee for the future. Nevertheless, Abraham obeyed and took Isaac up the mountain, built an altar to the Lord, and bound the boy to it just as God requested.

I can only imagine what this moment must have been like for Abraham holding the knife above his son. Gazing into the eyes of the son Abraham waited so long to see only for God to ask him to sacrifice him as a testament of Abraham's faith in God's providence.

At the last possible second, God's voice thundered:

"Do not lay a hand on the boy," he said. "Do not do anything to him. Now I know that you fear God, because you have not withheld from me your son, your only son." Genesis 22:12 NIV

An unstoppable rush of emotion and relief must have filled Abraham as he looked up from the altar and spotted a ram caught in a thicket nearby. God provides.

He always has. He always will.

"I swear by myself, declares the Lord, that because you have done this and have not withheld your son, your only son, I will surely bless you and make your descendants as numerous as the stars in the sky and as the sand on the seashore. Your descendants will take possession of the cities of their enemies, and through your offspring all nations on earth will be blessed, because you have obeyed me." Genesis 22:16-18 NIV

God trusted Abraham because Abraham trusted God. And because Abraham trusted God, God blessed Abraham beyond comprehension.

After our bout in Page, UT, I can better relate to Abraham and Sarah. Was our van getting stuck in the sand equal to their struggle for fertility? Nope. Was my promise to Alix that God was working in our situation anywhere close to God's promise to Abraham that God would make him a great nation through his one and only son, Isaac? Not even close. Was the faith required to stay positive as our entire trip and all our belongings teetered on the side of a sandy path in Utah equivalent to the faith needed to climb up a mountain offering the one thing he'd longed for his entire existence as a sacrifice of faith? Of course not.

But it's the closest I've come.

While the circumstances might be vastly different between Abraham and Sarah and Alix and me, one thing remains the same:

We all had no choice but to laugh.

Abraham and Sarah saw themselves in the mirror and laughed because they knew it would take a miracle for them to conceive. Alix and I—mainly I—saw our van up to its axles in the sand, ready to tip over at any second, and we laughed because we too knew it would take a miracle to free us.

But in both cases, God provided a solution. In fact, God is still making good on his promise to Abraham to this day.

Throughout the past four thousand years, Abraham's descendants have become numerous indeed. Through Christ's death on the cross for our sins, the family line is extended to include all who believe. Galatians 3:29 NIV

Through the adoption Paul describes in this verse from Galatians, Abraham's descendants are as numerous as the sand on the seashore and the stars in the sky, just as he promised. God fulfilled his promise to Abraham in the past through Abraham's son, Isaac. Likewise, God is fulfilling his promise to Abraham today through God's own son, Jesus.

The fulfillment of Abraham's promise has never been more apparent to me than that night on Lone Rock Beach. I quietly crawled out of the truck bed and onto my feet. I walked a few yards from the camp and felt God's peace once more.

I reached down to the ground and let delicate grains of sand run through my fingers on that Utah lakeshore. Then, I looked up and lost myself trying to count the shimmering stars clustered in the endless bands of the Milky Way.

The God of creation was fulfilling the 4000-year-old promise in front of my very eyes. All I had to do was be still.

God provides. He always has, and he always will.

F.A.V.O.R. DISCUSSION QUESTIONS
CHAPTER 12

Foundation: Genesis 22:12-15 "'Do not lay a hand on the boy,'" he said. 'Do not do anything to him. Now I know that you fear God, because you have not withheld from me your son, your only son.' Abraham looked up and there in a thicket he saw a ram[a] caught by its horns. He went over and took the ram and sacrificed it as a burnt offering instead of his son. So Abraham called that place The Lord Will Provide. And to this day it is said, 'On the mountain of the Lord it will be provided.'"

Application: In what area(s) of your life are you reliant on God today?

Vision: What sacrifices do you anticipate making in the future?

Orientation: To whom in your life is this story relevant? Write their name down and share it with them.

Name: _____

Reflection: Think back on your life. How does one of your experiences connect with Abraham's?

conclusion

I won't lie; I find it strange to have this book completed finally.

I have been telling people about the book for months, and I have been writing the manuscript for years. It required both more and less time, effort, and energy than I expected. Some days, I'd type for hours on end, and it seemed as if I could finish it all in a matter of days. Other days I had no motivation at all, and it seemed as if I'd never finish.

Whether I know you personally or not, I sincerely hope you decide to write a memoir of your own one day. Regardless of whether you want to write it or not, I hope you write a memoir. If for nothing else, I want you to write it to experience the highs and lows, the joys and pains, and ultimately, the incredible satisfaction of knowing your stories exist outside your own head, and that they won't die with you.

As I mentioned in the "How to Read This Book" section, I have some exciting updates to share. At the time of writing, each chapter seemed to have a conclusion; however, God is still continuing to write many of these stories today. I'll update the chapters in no particular order, and any chapters unmentioned do not have a further update at the time of publication.

Remember Skarleth Ayala from chapter eight?

Unfortunately, Skarleth decided to step away from her training to pursue an associate degree in psychology. Before she left NSPIRE, she painted a wonderful image of Russell, her instructor, and me in front of an airplane as a gift to us. The painting still hangs on the wall of the flight school.

Choosing psychology over aviation was difficult for Skarleth; however, she found psychology more immediately beneficial to her family as another income stream. Skarleth recently completed her associate degree and has intentions to return to the flight school when she has the financial means to do so. Her GoFundMe page is still active for those who would like to contribute to her training.

Please consider donating at gofund.me/29a3e200.

Speaking of the flight school, NSPIRE has "taken off!" Throughout the past couple of years, NSPIRE has seen a tremendous uptick in demand. We now have three aircraft, multiple students, and an incredible team of instructors. NSPIRE also moved into a new, bigger office space inside the Globe Building, and we sublease our old office spaces to other aviation-related startups. Russell and his family manage the daily operations of the flight school in my absence.

Remember Trevor from the lighting company in chapter eight? Trevor and I haven't worked together since our days at the lighting company, but we have remained best friends since. He is as close to me as a brother, and I can't imagine my life without him. I plan to have him be the best man at my wedding. I guess he'll find out when he reads this book!

Anyway, Trevor and his incredible wife, Kathryn, play so many roles in my life. During the pandemic, God blessed them with a beautiful baby boy named Ryder. Ryder overflows with joy and has an unforgettable smile.

I never knew I could love a child as much as I do Ryder.

After leaving the lighting company that brought us together, Trevor started and grew his own lighting company, using the profits to fund his passion project of composite materials. I am proud to say my family and I were the very first investors of his new company. Trevor and his team have garnered great interest thus far, and we are all very encouraged by their success. To infinity and beyond!

Finally, remember everyone's favorite World War II Veteran, Bowdre, from chapter two? At the time of writing, Bowdre is 98 years old and lives in a retirement home in McComb, Mississippi. He survived the COVID-19 pandemic and still stays very active. My parents visit him at least once a quarter. I try to visit at least once per year. I most recently visited in April 2021 enroute to a cousin's wedding in New Orleans.

A friend of mine, Daniel Ellender, has a unique gift for videography, photography, and storytelling. Bowdre is increasing in age, so I set up a time for Daniel and me to interview Bowdre in McComb. Bowdre requested that we all keep our masks on for the interview since we weren't fully vaccinated yet. If you'd like to watch the full interview, visit Daniel's company's website www.carpemomentumnow.com.

During the interview, Bowdre shared a bit about his experiences during the war; however, he said he chooses to die with most of his war stories for one reason or another. I didn't pry.

Since he wouldn't share many stories from the past, I changed the subject to the future. What was Bowdre looking forward to in his final days?

Bowdre's response struck me. "There's nothing left for me here."

While it might seem sad, his answer is an unfortunate truth in his world. What Bowdre was alluding to was that he is ready to die. His statement was reminiscent of my 92-year-old grandfather on his deathbed. Dr. Winters wanted to die, but he couldn't. Instead, he suffered.

No one wants to die until living becomes worse than death.

By the time we want to die, living is the only thing we still must do.

Bowdre and I had never talked about faith before. I took his striking comment as an opportunity to see where his head and heart were.

"Bowdre, if you think there's nothing left for you in this life, does that excite you about what is to come in the next life?" I asked.

"No, not really," Bowdre replied.

"Well, are you scared of dying? Or are you confident going into it?" I asked.

Bowdre paused for a second and then said, "I'm comfortable with it. But I don't know what happens to us when we die. I don't think anyone actually knows where we go when we die."

Before this question, I had been nodding my head to nearly every one of Bowdre's answers in affirmation. When he answered this question, he noticed I was no longer nodding.

Bowdre looked me in the eyes, paused, broke eye contact, thought to himself for a second, and repeated his remark; this time, less confident than the first.

"Yeah, I don't think anyone knows where we go when we die," he said, pausing for a moment more, before asking me the question, "Do you know where we go when we die?"

What a question.

Here was my opportunity to speak life into a man statistically on the threshold of death. I'd be lying if I said it didn't intimidate me.

"Well, Bowdre, Daniel, and I are Jesus followers. We take Jesus at his word when he said that if we believe in and follow him, we get to live for eternity in Heaven with him after we die. Now, I can't tell you where Heaven physically is, but I am confident Heaven is where I'm going when I die.

I also know that everything in Heaven, from golden streets to the pearly gates, all pales in comparison to merely being in the presence of Jesus. Heaven isn't the prize; Christ is."

This response took Bowdre back a bit, but it didn't unsettle him. My statement wasn't what he expected, but it also made him curious.

Finally, I added, "Bowdre, there is a lot I don't know, but one thing I know for certain is that Heaven wouldn't be the same without you in it." And I left it at that.

We continued the interview for an hour and a half before wrapping up. I asked to pray over Bowdre at the end, and he gladly accepted my offer. As soon as I said "Amen," the camera battery died. Not a second before or a second after.

God's timing is always perfect.

Daniel and I said our goodbyes and traveled to New Orleans. Three days later, Alix and I drove home to Atlanta. My parents were also going back to their home in West Monroe, Louisiana, and McComb, Mississippi, is on the way. They stopped by to see Bowdre.

After their visit, I got a call from my dad.

"We had a great visit with Bowdre. He was in such good spirits and loved the interview you and Daniel did. Your mom and I talked with him for a couple of hours today, and we could tell he spent the weekend thinking hard about what you guys discussed. We got to share our testimonies with him and tell him more about Jesus. In the end, we asked him if he'd like to pray the prayer of salvation and accept Jesus. He said he did. We prayed with him and over him, and it was one of the most memorable moments of my life. Thank you for starting the conversation. We'll all get to spend eternity with Bowdre because you did."

Bowdre talked a lot about legacy in our interview.

The one question I wish I had asked Bowdre that day but didn't is, "Why do you think God let you live to be 97 years old?"

Bowdre might not have known at the time. He still might not know. But I know that God has been loving, searching, and seeking Bowdre for 97 years, and thankfully God never gave up.

If you're reading this right now, it means God hasn't given up on you yet either. The question becomes: What has he left you here to do?

People talk and think about legacy a lot. As we grow older, our legacy becomes an increasing reality. How will you be remembered? Did you make your life count? What will people say about you at your funeral?

I've always said you can tell what a person believes about the next life by the way they live this one. How are you living?

What we do, how we live, and most importantly, who we live for on Earth, will determine what we do, how we live, and who we live with for eternity.

When you look back at your life with this book in mind, how will you live differently moving forward?

I have high hopes for you. After reading this book, I hope you don't simply put it on the shelf to collect dust. I hope you will use it as a guide to discover your own story filled with your own experiences tied to your own biblical parallels. You might have never opened a Bible, much less read any of it. I hope this book gives you a reason to.

I hope this book causes you to enjoy and appreciate your existence more than you did before. More than anything, I hope this book inspires you to be an active participant in the story God is writing in your life and to seek out opportunities where you've never looked for them.

If the exercise of writing this book has taught me anything, it is this: I should be much more concerned with what God says about me when I arrive in Heaven than what people say about me when I leave Earth.

I love words. If it weren't for words, I wouldn't be able to write this book and share my life with you through it. But as much as I cherish words, only seven count.

When this life is said and done, all that matters are the words "Well done, my good and faithful servant." (Matt 25:23 NIV)

I don't know what it will be like to enter into the presence of God, but I'm confident that is what I will hear when I get there. Not because I'm a better person than anyone else. Not because I'm any holier or more religious than my peers, but because Christ gave everything for me by dying for my sins, and I'm using this life as my best attempt to repay the favor.

God doesn't need to use me. God doesn't need to use you either. But he allows us to be used by him to accomplish his purposes. This truth represents one of the greatest gifts of this life. While it's great, it is not the greatest gift.

The greatest gift of all—even above salvation itself— is free will.

As much as God loved you to give his only son in exchange, he loved you that much more to provide you with the right to deny and reject that love. What a loving God he is. I pray this book and the accounts within encourage you to seek God because he is knocking down the doors seeking you. I hope this book is one tool he's using to do so.

Every other religion is man's attempt to get to God.

Christianity is God's attempt to get to man.

Are you that man or woman God is seeking today?

I'll be honest, I wrestled with keeping the next section in this book. Part of me wanted to scrap it in fear that it might diminish the story or distract from the narrative.

Kind of selfish now that I'm looking back.

I decided to keep it, and I'm confident in that decision.

What good is a message without a call to action? What good is a race if you only run to the finish line, not through it?

Well, here's your call to action. Here's your finish line.

When death greets you, are you sure you'll spend eternity in Heaven? Are you confident that you'll hear those precious seven words "Well done, my good and faithful servant"?

If you aren't, I'd like to invite you to say a prayer with me. But first, I must warn you.

Anyone who tells you becoming a Jesus follower will make your life easier is lying to you. In fact, if you're doing it right, following Jesus will cost you. For some, following Jesus cost them their jobs. For others, following Jesus cost them everything they own. For the disciples, following Jesus cost them their lives.

Following Jesus won't make your life easier, but it will make your life better. He will make you better because by following Jesus, you become more like him.

By accepting Jesus as your Lord and Savior, you give his spirit immediate consent to dwell inside of your heart. Your life from that point forward is not your own; instead, it is Christ living through you. Only Jesus's followers can experience the confidence and peace that Christ purchased for them on the cross. The assurance that the pain and struggle of this world are temporary, and the best in life is yet to come. Could you use this confidence today?

If so, pray this prayer with me.

"Father, I come to you today, a sinner in need of a savior. Thank you for your mercy and for sending your son, Jesus, to take the full penalty of my sin on the cross even though I don't deserve it. I ask that you fill me with your spirit and reveal yourself to me in mighty ways. Today, I surrender my life to you."

If you earnestly prayed this prayer, today marks the most significant turning point in human life. (Romans 10:9-10)

Congratulations! To be "born again" in Christ outweighs even your first birth. I hope you will mark this day in your calendar and celebrate it as much as you do your physical birthday. We want to celebrate with you and support you in your walk, so please email us at theartofeverythingbook@gmail.com to let us know it's your re-birthday!

From now on, you aren't just living for the temporal; you are living for the eternal. Your story isn't just your own, but his story written through you. Your life on Earth isn't less valuable because you have another one waiting for you in Heaven. Instead, it is more valuable now that you know how much is on the line!

But don't forget that you can't earn your way into Heaven. You'll never be good enough to get there on your own, so don't try to be. Your deeds are a result of your salvation, not a requirement.

Want to know the coolest part about Heaven? You get unlimited guest passes! People are the only thing you can bring to Heaven with you, so start sharing the good news with them.

One easy way to do this is to send a copy of this book to someone you love. If you completed the F.A.V.O.R. discussion questions at the end of each chapter, you already have a tailor-made list of twelve people! If you haven't answered those questions yet, consider going back and doing so. I'm confident God will place the right people on your heart with whom to share the good news.

Don't miss out on this incredible opportunity.

My friend, Dakota, shared a story with me which will stay with me forever. Jesus says at the end of time will be a wide path and a narrow path. (Matt 7:13-14) The wide path leads to destruction, but the narrow path leads to life. Many more will be on the wide path than the narrow.

Dakota's fear, as it should be for us all, is as we stand on the narrow path, we would glance over and see friends or family looking across at us from the wide path saying, "You knew this the whole time, and you never said anything."

If that scares you, some conversations in your life need to take place. Ask yourself these two questions:

Who do you love enough to bring to Heaven with you?

Who do you hate enough to keep Heaven from?

Wrestle with these as you begin to see, think, act, believe, trust, follow, and live eternally. "The old is gone; the new has come." (2 Corinthians 5:17 NIV)

You are all in all a new creation. But how can you be new if you still have a past?

Your past is redeemed. Christ purchased our regrets, mistakes, and sin by his death on the cross, and now you and I get to use our past to bring life to other people through him.

Do you have regrets? Here is your chance to start over. Have you missed out on life, lacking the courage to live it? Here is your chance to make it right.

Identify the various gifts and instruments God's uniquely given you to use for this challenge. What talents, traits, or abilities are you aware of or have others noticed in you? Use them to speak life into others.

What pain, loss, addiction, depression, or abuse have you suffered that could provide hope to someone going through something similar? Use them to speak life into others.

Much of my story is found within the covers of this book. Much more is not. I've experienced my share of pain, loss, addiction, depression, and abuse like you. A lot of what I've experienced thus far I wouldn't ask to experience again. But now that I have been there, I can empathize with and speak life into others.

The very events or situations I thought God was using to punish me resulted in the greatest gifts he ever gave me. Your mess is your message.

Don't waste it. Wear it as a badge of honor instead of covering it like a scar. Flip the script on your past. God gave us the perfect example of how to do this. Jesus's defeat on the cross was his ultimate victory. Through death, God gave us eternal life. What was meant for evil, God always uses for good.

Jesus wears his scars proudly, and so should we.

Each wound is the building block of your testimony. Incorporate them into the rest of your canvas. Don't limit yourself to your own canvas. Your calling is much greater than that. It's time to look at the bigger picture. Open your eyes to see how your work fits with the rest of the canvases God is weaving together as his eternal masterpiece. This is what it means to connect your story to History.

We are all but one small, yet incredibly significant grain of sand on a never-ending seashore. We are one tiny, yet brilliantly twinkling star in a boundless cosmos of light, created to reflect and bring glory to the one who made us.

This is your story. This is your time. I pray that you make the most of both.

Own it. Live it. Share it.

Your story + my story = History

CPSIA information can be obtained
at www.ICGtesting.com
Printed in the USA
LVHW052018080322
712946LV00013B/544

9 798985 466102